Discovering Your Child's Design

Discovering Your Child's Design

RALPH MATTSON AND THOM BLACK

LIFEJOURNEY
BOOKS

David C. Cook Publishing Co.
Elgin, Illinois   Weston, Ontario

LifeJourney Books is an imprint of David C. Cook Publishing Co.
David C. Cook Publishing Co., Elgin Illinois 60120
David C. Cook Publishing Co., Weston, Ontario

Edited by Stan Campbell
Design (cover and interior) by Dawn Lauck
Technical presentation by April Frost
Production by Steve Johnson

DISCOVERING YOUR CHILD'S DESIGN

First Printing, 1989
Printed in the United States of America
94 93 92 91 90 89 5 4 3 2 1

Mattson, Ralph.
        Discovering Your Child's Design / Ralph Mattson and Thom Black.
                p.   cm.
        ISBN 1-55513-226-X
        1. Child rearing.   I. Black, Thom.   II. Title.
        HQ769.M3685   1989b
        649´.1—dc20   89-32705

Table of Contents

Dedication

To Carolyn,
    Karyn Ruth,
        David Brian,
            Glenn Eric,
                and Lynn Anne

And to Deborah,
        Joshua David,
            Talia Joy,
                and Megan Elyse

Introduction

I have fathered four children. I should be accustomed to the process by now, but I must confess that I still find the whole business quite extraordinary. In terms of accomplishments, no other event in my life even approaches the significance of being involved in the creation of new persons.

I realized this fact the very first time I heard I was to be a father. The news was delivered by a breathless wife who was trying to conceive a picture in her head of what already had been conceived in her body . . . a new personality! Both of us went through the mental gymnastics of imagining what a new individual would look like . . . act like . . . think like.

A few months later, the matter was no longer abstract. Clear physical evidence had emerged. Someone was reshaping my wife's body into rather ludicrous proportions.

A new parent's awe: How can a person suddenly exist where there was not one before?

tremendous *adj* : **1** : being such as to make one tremble; terrifying **2.** (Colloq.) very large; great; enormous; wonderful; amazing; extraordinary.

Infants believe the role of parents should be that of personal servants whose attentions should focus only on them.

Inches away from our exploring hands was an entirely new person—kicking and moving about in a bulbous, liquid world of its own. This was a phenomenon of major importance to us, filled with mysteries so vast that our knowledge of sex and physiology made little difference. It was not merely a matter of novelty. It was, in every sense of the word, tremendous.

Our awestruck reaction to our first child was repeated at the birth of our second. And our third. And our fourth. It didn't lessen as our infants became toddlers, as our toddlers became youngsters, and as they too swiftly became adults. During all those years we never could get accustomed to the wonder of being parents.

Now lest you think my wife and I are a couple of sentimentalists, be assured that we are quite aware that infants, so cutely portrayed in magazine articles and television ads, are completely uncivilized. Their only concerns are their own creaturely comforts. Infants may look cherubic and often act accordingly, but basically they want what they want, in spite of whatever needs others may have—and they always want it immediately. The world and everyone in it exists for their convenience and pleasure. They have little regard for anyone else's concerns, possessions, or time. It requires years of training and education to civilize them as our parents civilized us.

In addition, we are quite aware that not all children will turn out well. We realize the risks involved. Children do not always become what we hope, even when our hopes are centered on what is clearly best for the child. They can make wrong choices and, too often, even bad choices. It is a nasty fact that the next generation of criminals will come from the ranks of children now with us.

Yet in spite of such vivid realities, our parental sense of wonder still persists. It is a glorious experience to have and to know children. Whatever gamble we took in becoming parents, if indeed it was a gamble, paid off marvelously.

This book contains some of what my wife and I have learned. I have also invited Thomas Black, as a younger parent, to add what he and his wife have experienced. Together we intend to equip other parents to approach their responsibilities with a clearer understanding of what they are doing. We want to enhance the ability of fathers and mothers to nurture and equip their children to live effectively in a strange and fallen world.

The risks of parenthood are well worth taking.

How can we accomplish this goal while realizing that we cannot deal with all aspects of child rearing in one book? We do feel we can introduce an important key which parents can use to unlock a number of doors which otherwise may stay closed. I refer to the fact of unique design within the human personality.

If Thom and I were the readers instead of the writers, our first reaction might be one of suspicion. After all, considering the many books which have already been written, the decades of research, the numbers of professionals who have spoken on these matters, isn't it presumptuous to claim that we can add something of significance?

Truthfully, can anything new be said about child rearing?

We acknowledge the possibility of such an attitude, but frankly, we do expect to make a useful contribution. And before you are done with these chapters, we also want to radically challenge your perceptions of your children and your role in parenting them. The proof, as the old-timers tell us, will be in the pudding.

Ralph T. Mattson
Canton Center, Connecticut

Why Didn't Jimmy Do His Homework

"Jimmy didn't do his homework."

"He didn't?"

"No, he didn't."

"Why not?"

"I don't know."

"You don't know?"

"I don't know."

"Well, *I* know," says the Doctor. "Jimmy is growing so quickly that he exhausts his energy quite easily. It has gotten to the point where his body naturally rebels and Jimmy, in desperation, has to quit. He needs rest from the pressures of homework. Leave him alone for a period of rest. Let him be."

"Are you serious?" asks the Theologian. "I say that Jimmy is a member of the fallen human race and we are seeing symptoms of his rebellion. If you let him be, all you

Leave Jimmy alone?

are doing is encouraging his basic sinful nature. Let Jimmy know that you will not tolerate such disobedience. Discipline is in order, not permissiveness!"

Give Jimmy some help?

"Come, come," says the Educator. "Let's not get carried away. Jimmy, after all, is just a little boy trying to deal with the multitudinous demands of school. He probably didn't quite understand the lesson and consequently is not able to do the assignment based on that lesson. What he really needs is a little remedial work. Then he will be OK."

"That's all very well and good," says the Researcher, "but it seems to me that you are suggesting cures and prescriptions based on limited data. Jimmy's IQ could be marginal and perhaps he is being stretched beyond his capacity. What he needs is testing in order for us to be sure."

Give Jimmy some tests?

"You may be right," says the Therapist, "but I would not limit the testing to merely the measurement of Jimmy's IQ. I recommend a battery of tests. Jimmy may have a learning disability and all we are seeing is the tip of the iceberg. He may need quite a bit of therapeutic work."

The Psychiatrist speaks up: "I am afraid you are all being too simplistic about this. I suspect that Jimmy is dealing with internal emotional pressures. His failure to do his homework is a signal to the adult world, from whom he expects support and guidance, that those interior confusions are too much to bear. What he requires is more than some educator's Band-Aids, misguided assessments, or parental coddling."

Give Jimmy a hug?

"Let's not get carried away with scientific mumbo jumbo," says the Counselor. "Jimmy needs support from outside the family—someone who won't threaten him with punishment, but will accept him on his own terms, just the way he is. An arm around the shoulder from someone who is not going to make any demands on him—that's what he needs."

"What is all this garbage?" exclaims Aunt Maude. "Did

you always do *your* homework when you were a kid? Maybe the reason little Jimmy didn't do his homework is because he simply didn't feel like doing it. Do you always feel like doing your work? Don't you ever have the urge to ignore your responsibilities? Do you expect him to be perfect? Leave the poor boy alone."

"Amen!" says Mrs. Johnson, a neighbor from the house across the street.

"Don't worry about it," says the Pastor. "It will all work out."

"Amen," says Mrs. Johnson, again.

"Jimmy didn't do his homework."

"Why didn't he do his homework?"

"I don't know."

"Neither do I."

HULLABALOO AND TUMULT

We can be sure, as modern parents, that any attempt to explain Jimmy's behavior will become a confusing matter as soon as we step outside our own opinions. All the "experts" on behavior have a lot to say, sometimes to our benefit. Yet too often their advice sounds like a confusion of conflicting theories. We also discover contrasts as we compare how one generation is brought up in comparison with others. One generation of children is brought up with rigid expectations of behavior and decorum, while another is noted for its permissiveness.

Perhaps as a child you had to be very selective about what you could talk about with adults. Today's children, however, are often free and open about what they discuss with us. All generations are blessed or victimized by the attitudes and theories that happen to be in fashion during their growing-up years. Consequently, no generation of parents should completely trust the "norm" that they believe to be true for their children. We should always question our assumptions.

When your child's welfare is at stake, whom can you believe?

A major goal of this book is to demonstrate that Christian parents don't consistently build on a biblical base.

As Christians, we might expect to be immune to the influence of current theories about why we and our children behave the way we do. After all, don't we base our child-rearing practices on biblical principles? Not always. Too often, without even knowing it, we yield to the influence of the world's confused way of looking at children.

Before we deal with some of these influences, we would first like to take a look at Jimmy (and subsequently your own child) in a fresh and different way. From this new perspective we can build a strategy of child rearing that will result in significant benefits to you and your children. And since it is biblical and practical, this perspective will also allow you to critique whatever advice comes your way—whether from the pulpit, the lectern, or your own school system.

Jimmy's advisers have a common flaw.

So if we return now to the dialogue surrounding little Jimmy's homework assignment, we recall lots of diversity in how different people would respond. They have one thing in common, though. They all focus solely on the problem itself. And for the duration of the problem, they all see Jimmy only in connection to it. He, in turn, will come to see himself in terms of the problem, which adds more fuel to the fire. And before long, trying to analyze why Jimmy does whatever he does becomes like trying to map out a plate of spaghetti.

TRYING A NEW SET OF SPECTACLES

"Teacher, this woman was caught in the act of adultery."

Jimmy's advisers need to look at him through a different set of glasses. His problem can be approached in a far more creative way by attempting to use principles adapted from the way Jesus Christ related to people. The New Testament contains a number of good examples, but we will refer to the well-known incident of the woman caught in the act of adultery (John 8:1-11). Remember that the religious leaders were rightly concerned about her serious behavior problem, and they questioned Jesus about how to handle it.

The Pharisees were actually trying to trap Jesus with the question they posed, but He knew their intentions. Jesus immediately contrasted the woman's sin with those of the Pharisees, which caused them to reconsider their proposed course of action.

"If any one of you is without sin, let him be the first to throw a stone at her."

Jesus also knew what was best for the woman. And in the face of the conflict, He maneuvered the situation to the point where she could be released and receive her freedom again.

Jesus didn't ignore the woman's problem. Rather, He told her to go and leave her life of sin. This story parallels the unutterable sweetness experienced by anyone who has been released from the guilt of sin—not by denying the reality of the sin, but by seeing it from God's view. The power of God's grace provides an entirely different perspective. It allows us to admit the reality—even the terrible danger—of a problem. It accomplishes the dual result of solving the difficulty while saving the person. And it goes further by building up the individual. In this story, the woman ended up with much more than a solution to a life-threatening problem.

"Has no one condemned you? Neither do I condemn you."

Jesus called His disciples using the same positive approach. Among them were peasant fishermen and a tax collector. Neither vocation could be perceived as adequate to the call, but Jesus vouched for who they *were* rather than what they weren't. He confidently called them into a new phase of living. And they trusted Him to live up to His promise, "I will make you fishers of men" (Matthew 4:19).

Jesus saw beyond appearances, beyond social and economic status. He saw people in terms of what they were created to be. He saw the gifts God had given people who did not have proper "credentials." Unfortunately, Jesus' exciting, supportive, winsome approach to people is not practiced by many of today's religious leaders.

The perspective Jesus had in dealing with the adulterous woman and in calling His disciples is characteristic of

Christianity at its best. Not by pretending that everyone is basically good, true, and beautiful. Not by ignoring discipline or the hard things in life. Not by encouraging people to develop some kind of fictional potential—as if you could possibly get gold by spinning straw or get apples from oak trees. Instead, we are shown the importance of looking at people according to the way God views them. Such an approach has the potential of liberating people and helping them experience what is best for them.

Getting back to little Jimmy, we suggest that more can be done for him than what we have seen so far. Previously, Jimmy's advisers were making the problem a window through which they saw him (from a limited perspective). They focused on what he is not doing and doesn't want to do.

We can do more for Jimmy when we imitate Christ and choose His gracious, positive approach. We should look at who Jimmy *is* and what he *does* do. Before we begin to deal with him as a defiant pupil, we shall look at his strengths.

Getting into Jimmy's World

An adult's evaluation of Jimmy's behavior is likely to depend on the person's perspective and the amount of information that has been gathered. If someone is interested only in reaching a conclusion about Jimmy's homework problem, then learning a few facts about Jimmy may lead to a "simple" solution. But Jimmy is more than a few basic facts; he is a whole world of his own. Anyone who recognizes this fact will probably discover that Jimmy is a complete, unified creation of such vivid detail that even the angels marvel at his design.

Of course, the angels know that Jimmy (like all of us) has been damaged by the fall of the human race from its original glory. But they are also aware of the original design and all that the Designer has done to restore us to Himself.

It's true that people in this world don't often see the wonder that Jimmy truly is. His parents and family do to

Jimmy was shaped in and by the mind of God.

some degree, but their attitude is merely due to the fact that he is theirs and they love him. A family is expected to appreciate its own members, yet even family members focus more on the exterior than the interior. They certainly do not see what the angels see. Jimmy's family tends to read his personality according to how well it conforms to what they want it to be. They have been trained to see him as raw material to be shaped by their influence.

In addition to his family, Jimmy must contend with the larger sphere of society, which tends to have a debased view of many of its own members. In too many places, society actually presumes the right to provide the means for obliterating any people like Jimmy who arrive at an inconvenient time or an undesired situation. They obviously see little if anything of Jimmy's true, magnificent nature.

Many times we are blocked from being able to fully appreciate individuals because of the sheer number of people in the world. We are incapable of seeing value in something which is so abundant. We become spiritually blind. And because it boggles our minds to think of billions of people as individuals, we end up comparing Jimmy the individual against the total population of the world as a whole. But an infinite God finds such a comparison foolish.

God knows every individual on the entire globe much more completely than any parent knowing one Jimmy. After all, each of us continues to be alive from moment to moment because God breathes life into us every moment. So we need to acknowledge God's sovereignty in respect to ourselves and our children.

We need to make decisive breaks from sloppy thinking and embrace reality. Who defines that reality? God does. Our Creator is the One who defines us and imparts value to each of us. So no matter how many of us there are in this world, we should see each other through the eyes of the One who created us. Consequently, those who know God should have a different perspective.

"Amid the millions upon millions of people on this planet," we ask, "how can one little Jimmy be important?"

I praise You because I am fearfully and wonderfully made; Your works are wonderful, I know that full well (Psalm 139:14).

God made Jimmy in the image of Himself. That fact allows us to assume that there are some things we can know about Jimmy by understanding the nature of God. We know about God's personality because of the way He has acted in the past. We can state that He is love because we have felt His love in our personal relationships with Him. We know He is just and that He is merciful in the same way. His character is not abstract. It has been translated into action throughout history. God acts according to who He is. When we perceive the pattern of God's behavior—the motif of His actions—we are able to make conclusions about His personality.

Similarly, we can discover the design of Jimmy's personality by looking at the consistent ways he has behaved during his lifetime. And knowing his design should add meaning to Jimmy's birthday celebrations, to our relationships with him, to the way we discipline and teach him, and to the way we communicate with him. Only after we have discovered his design can we begin to understand how we can best go about helping him with his homework problem. Later, when he is older and when the available information is more comprehensive, we will be able to give him the most accurate educational and career advice possible. But for now, we need not be so ambitious. All we need to discover at this point is enough to encourage and nurture Jimmy according to his own nature.

Discovering a child's design should influence our actions and attitudes toward him or her.

READER REBUTTAL?

Let us pause here and deal with a question that you are likely to have. At our seminars, we are often challenged at this point about what we have said. It usually goes something like this:

Wait a minute. Before you proceed any further, you need to know that I have a problem with your approach. I agree that it is right to discover something about the nature of man by looking at God, who created man in His image.

God's behavior is one thing, because it is consistent. Yet a person's behavior is affected radically by sin, so it is not a pure basis for evaluation. Human behavior is unreliable because it comes out of confused motives. Then you also have to consider that Jimmy is just a kid, a beginner doing all kinds of things haphazardly. How can you conclude anything with so many variables?

I prefer to start with basic assumptions before we get to the really complex issues. Certainly human behavior can never duplicate the perfection of God. If it could, there would be no reason for this book because we would all have a clear understanding of each other's method of operating. We would also appreciate each other a lot more than we do now.

Granted, each of us presents a confusing picture of mixed motives. However, each individual still reveals quite a bit about himself if you know what to look for. So first let's take a peek at a portion of Jimmy's hidden world and learn some elementary facts. Later we will tackle the more complicated implications of the problem you presented.

REVEALING
S·T·O·R·I·E·S

For the most part, Jimmy's world is a hidden one. It is hidden even from the people who are closest to him—his family. Jimmy's parents assume his world is being fully developed under their care. And yes, he does feel their influence as he grows. Yet parents sometimes don't understand that Jimmy has a head start on them.

At birth, Jimmy is a unique, complex being—already designed by God. Whatever happens to him beyond that point either reinforces or works against his special design. This explains why all children don't react the same way in response to their parents and environment.

This is one of the peculiarities of being a modern parent. We are taught that children are like putty to be shaped by our influence. If we do the right things, we get certain results. Yet our children do not respond like putty nor do they behave similarly. We are taught one thing in theory and know something completely different by experience.

One of the most revealing windows into this reality comes from contrasting the actions and responses of children raised in the same home. Observing how a brother and sister approach similar opportunities with vastly different intentions proves the diversity of behavior even when they have been raised with the same values and the same domestic policies! Rarely do two children ever approach a situation the same way. So let's take another look at Jimmy, this time in contrast to his sister, Talia.

[NOTE: At this point we should reveal that "Jimmy" is actually Joshua, son of author Thom Black. The previous stories and the ones that follow are all true, and are told from Thom's perspective.]

LEARNING HOW TO RIDE A BIKE

Jimmy's approach—Jimmy pestered us to death to get him a bike. Living in an area with no good bicycle routes, I held out until he was seven and then got him one for his birthday. Right away, it became the focal point of our time together. He wasn't immediately able to balance on two wheels, so the bike sat around for a few weeks with him being unable to ride it. Finally, he asked for my help. So together, hand in hand, we walked to the garage. Out came the bike, up went Jimmy, and down the street we went (with me running and him riding). At last, after many days, Jimmy learned to ride the bike. And I had run several miles.

Talia's approach—Talia was four when she decided she wanted a bike. With Jimmy riding all around, Talia announced she wanted to learn how to ride, too. Four-year-old girls are little, tiny things and I didn't want to buy a little, tiny, brand-new bike which she would only use for one summer. We found an ad for a used bike in the newspaper. We bought it and it came complete with training wheels. Once we had the bike home, up and down the driveway she would go. As I watched, I dreaded the day

Dad, are you busy? I want to ride my bike.

Go ahead.

Come on, Dad. You know you have to help me.

Can you practice by yourself until I get there?

No, that's OK. I'll wait for you.

when she would be too big for the training wheels. I didn't look forward to those additional miles to run.

A few weeks later I looked outside and saw Talia standing over Jimmy, instructing him in the removal of her training wheels. Nuts and bolts were strewn all over the driveway. There was no doubt left that Talia wanted those wheels off. When Jimmy finished, Talia picked up her bike, got on, went a few feet, and fell off. She got back on, went a few more feet, and fell off again. And she kept repeating the process until she was riding. All by herself. No miles for me to run!

WORKBOOKS

Jimmy's approach—From the first day we placed a workbook in front of Jimmy, he had no difficulty doing pages and pages at a time. Some weekends he would finish 75 pages at a crack. Other times he wouldn't go near it. What we couldn't get a handle on was *when* he would want to work in his workbook and when he wouldn't. Eventually we noticed a pattern.

When his mother or I were around, he would sometimes sit and work for hours at a time. The instant we got up, Jimmy would vanish. When we returned to the table, Jimmy would reappear. Up, he's gone. Down, he's back. Workbook after workbook has been completed by Jimmy when we were *together* at the table. Open any page and I can tell you what I was doing when Jimmy worked on it.

Talia's approach—Talia's involvement with workbooks wasn't shrouded in quite as much mystery as Jimmy had allowed us to experience.

Where is Talia?
Downstairs working on her workbook.
Talia, what do you like about working in your
    workbook?
Doing it.
Enough said.

Jimmy, why don't you work in your workbook?
I don't really want to.
What do you like about working in your workbook?
What I like most is finishing it and spending time with you.
Come on. I'll sit at the table with you.
OK.

SHOPPING

Jimmy's approach—We have one of two distinct expectations every time we enter a shopping mall, depending on whether the trip includes Jimmy or Talia. Jimmy is interested in the *deal*.

> *Dad, can we buy something?*
> We don't need anything.
> *But Dad, maybe something is on sale.*
> I don't care.
> *But Dad, we should look and see if there is anything we can use!*
> I don't want to buy anything.
> *But Dad! Let's just see.*

And so I will walk through the mall, having to offer hundreds of explanations to Jimmy as to why we are deciding not to take advantage of all the money-saving opportunities available to us.

Talia's approach—Talia makes us a nervous wreck whenever we take her to the mall. Shopping is usually the farthest thing from her mind. She's an explorer, and we have had several frantic moments as we realize she has wandered off.

We often find her standing with another family, surrounded by other children as if she belonged. The mother is usually talking to her children when we reach in and grab Talia, and is startled that Talia has crept in without her noticing.

> Where is Talia?
> *I don't know. She was here a minute ago.*
> TALIA! TALIA, WHERE ARE YOU!? [We eventually find her.]
> Sweetheart, you can't wander off like that. Please stay close.
> *OK, Dad.*
> Debbie, let's go home . . . Where is Talia?
> *I don't know. She was here a minute ago.*

Jimmy, what do you like about going to the mall?
Buying stuff.

Talia, what do you like about going to the mall?
I like listening to people.

PLAYING

Megan's approach—Jimmy and Talia have a two-year-old sister, Megan. By now, you shouldn't be surprised to discover that she isn't like either of her siblings. Megan spends much of her time taking care of her "children."

> Where did all these dolls come from?
> *Megan got them out.*
> There must be ten of them.
> *I know. She is taking care of them.*
> Is that why she has them all lined up on the floor?
> *Yes. She has nursed them all and put them to sleep.*
> Did Talia ever do that?
> *Never.*

Jimmy's approach—Coming home late one night after everyone was in bed, I walked through the dark living room on the way to the bedroom. I could feel something brushing against my feet, so I flipped on the light to see what was on the floor. Turning around, I could see that my last five steps had taken me through a floor full of paper airplanes that apparently had been arranged in some sort of squadron detail.

I knew instinctively that if those planes were messed up when someone woke up in the morning, I was in big trouble. So at 1:00 A.M. I spent ten minutes on my hands and knees placing paper airplanes in neat, tight rows. Finished, I continued on to bed.

> *Dad? Hey, Dad?*
> My eyes flicker open. It's 6:00 A.M. "What?" I say. The word gags in my throat.
> *Did you see my airplanes?*
> Uh-huh.
> *There are ninety of them.*
> Ninety paper airplanes?
> *Yeah. Aren't they cool?*

Jimmy removes the paper airplanes from the living room floor and places them in a heap in his room, where

Tell me about the airplanes.
Well, first I made one. Then I wanted more, so I made another one. Then I wanted more, so I kept making them until I ran out of paper.

they remain for several more days. He eventually collects them in a large garbage bag and deposits them in the trash. The paper airplanes are never played with.

CLEANING UP

Talia's approach—It's not surprising to find the kids' rooms messy. One evening in particular, Talia's room was in sad shape. Almost everything she owned was either on the floor or in some semblance of a pile. At about seven in the evening, I asked her to make her room neat. Away she went, with her door closing behind her. At eight-thirty, I knocked on her door.

Talia? It's time to get ready for bed.

OK.

I tried to open the door. So much stuff was on the floor that I had to put my shoulder against the door to get in. As I looked around, I couldn't see that one thing had been touched. Piles of everything imaginable were scattered all over her room. What had she done for over an hour?

I looked down and saw that Talia was just finishing putting the last pair of socks in a drawer which she had emptied out when she had gone into her room. I looked into the drawer and could see that it was immaculate, every piece of clothing folded neatly and placed exactly where it was supposed to go. She looked up at me and closed her drawer with a huge smile on her face.

I am all finished with my room, Dad.

Talia's approach vs. Jimmy's approach—One evening Jimmy and Talia had been given the task of cleaning up the basement, but they had absolutely no desire whatsoever to do so. After seeing the exaggerated panic and pain all over their faces, I strategically tried to make a game out of it. I set the stove timer for twenty minutes and challenged them to see if they could finish in the allotted time.

Jimmy's eyes narrowed into slits, sizing up the situation. Then he looked at Talia, their eyes met, and they both

What did you like about cleaning up your drawer? I like the way it looks when it is finished.

exploded down the stairs. I immediately grew pleased with myself in the clever way that I was going to get the basement cleaned up.

Eighteen minutes later Jimmy raced up the stairs, said the basement was all done, and wondered if he had beaten the timer. When I told him he had two minutes to spare, he said that if he got a reward he wanted ice cream for dessert. Then he disappeared into his room as I looked at my wife with a pleased, *I-am-in-control* look on my face.

Fifteen minutes later, Talia appeared from below and also assured me that the basement was all clean. She sat down at the table and began to arrange her silverware around her while I checked out this project. As I walked downstairs, I was simply amazed. The room was still wall-to-wall toys and showed little evidence of being touched. But I have to say that the kids had left their mark.

Jimmy had risen to the challenge of completing the basement in under twenty minutes by starting at the stairs and cleaning a straight, but very narrow path through all the toys. He had tossed playthings this way and that, until he reached the far side of the basement. His project took about eighteen minutes, and when he finished it looked as if someone had drawn a giant bull's-eye on that far wall for him to hit. Had he finished? Yes. Had he cleaned up? Not on your life.

Talia's efforts were less noticeable. The basement was still a mess and she had been down here a lot longer than Jim. I looked around and my eye caught an old, play kitchen set we had rescued out of someone's trash five years ago that was now in the far corner of the basement. The only way to get to it was to walk on top of several thousand toys and try not to break your neck.

The kitchen was an amazing sight. It was immaculate. A dozen little bottles were placed in tidy rows. Play knives and forks were all arranged in neat, little stacks. I opened the oven doors and saw all of her pots and pans in their

I'll tell you what. I'll set this timer on the stove for twenty minutes. Let's see if you can get the basement cleaned up before the timer dings.
Do we get anything?
We'll see.

Jimmy, what were you thinking as you cleaned the basement?
I wanted to beat the timer before it went off.
How did you clean?
I picked up as many toys as fast as I could until I got to the other end of the basement. Then I ran upstairs.
What did you like about that adventure?
Beating the timer, but I was hoping I would get a prize, like ice cream.

Talia, what were you thinking as you cleaned the basement?

I thought the kitchen looked the messiest, so that's what I cleaned up.

How did you clean up the kitchen?

First I took everything out. Then I put all the same things together—the knives and forks, the pots and dishes, and stuff like that. When I was all done, there were a bunch of bottles left, so I lined them up on top.

What did you like most about cleaning up your kitchen?

The way it looked when it was finished.

proper places. Dozens of accessories were all right where they were supposed to be. What a good job she had done! What a messy basement I had to straighten up.

SPENDING TIME WITH DAD

I had to make a short trip to the mall. My wife suggested I take Talia along with me. Even at five years old, Talia always seems to be busy with her friends or doing some other activity that doesn't involve the family. She never seems to be interested in being included like Jimmy does. Jimmy loves to do things—anything at any time. But Talia needs more encouragement.

After a few silent moments to consider all her options, Talia finally agrees to go with me. As we pull out of the driveway, I can see Jimmy playing football with three friends. As soon as he realizes that I'm headed out, he leaves the game and runs for the car. Simultaneously, Talia notices two friends walking around the corner toward our house. At the exact moment Jimmy leaps into the backseat, Talia bounces out the front door, squealing, "There are Colleen and Heather!" My head whirls from side to side. In the blink of an eye, I have switched children.

This swap floated around in my head for days, for it vividly illustrated one of the major differences between my children. I have had the opportunity to communicate freely and frequently with Jimmy because he is always there. We talk about everything because he is constantly next to me. He knows what I think about a lot of things.

Talia is different. She is always busy with personal activities or with her friends. Our times together are irregular and much less frequent. In fact, if I don't make an effort to penetrate her world, we can go for days without spending time together. As a father and a friend, I need to be much more thoughtful in how I interact with Talia.

As you consider your involvement with your own child or children, you need to be ready to respond to each person's unique design. One strategy will not work for every child—even when children are brother and sister. With this in mind, let's work on some things that will help you create an appropriate strategy for each child you want to reach. The next chapter will help you come to some simple, but useful, conclusions—including the elusive answer as to why Jimmy didn't do his homework.

In reviewing the history of nations, you often hear a reference to the principle that *the past is the best predictor of the future*. The same principle holds true when looking at the history of individual lives. We have tracked a small portion of the histories of Jimmy, Talia, and Megan, and we have made a number of observations concerning their behavior. As we begin to understand their actions, we become more equipped to respond in ways which make the most sense for each of them.

The things that have been said so far about children are actually true about everyone. All of us enjoy some things and situations, and we dislike others. In fact, the authors' guidelines for discovering a person's design are derived from an assessment technology used professionally by the authors to enable organizations to select the right people and manage them wisely, for church management and career

We all are drawn naturally or even propelled into making moves because of certain ideas or intentions which we enjoy or for which we have an affinity.

development (*MOTIF Assessment by the DOMA Institute*, © 1988, by Ralph Mattson). In such situations, considerably more information is usually needed than is required by parents working with young children. But keep in mind that it is possible to go into a wealth of detail when working with teenagers and adults. You can enrich your understanding to whatever degree is useful for a given situation.

Perhaps the material in this book has reminded you of some of your own situations. As you move ahead, keep those specific examples in mind. When we deal with how best to handle Jimmy, Talia, and Megan, make appropriate notations for how you can use the information in regard to the people you know. And as we promised, we're going to find out why Jimmy didn't do his homework.

DIFFERENCES AND DISTINCTIONS

We mentioned at the end of the last chapter that Jimmy needs to continually cultivate contact with Talia. By nature, she doesn't have the same need for people that Jimmy does. Sure, both she and Jimmy talk around the dinner table and go through the normal chitchat of family life. But Jimmy, by nature, will engage others to do lots of other things with him—whether sports, learning how to ride, or doing homework. Talia won't.

Parents could misunderstand if they evaluate Talia from the perspective of popular psychology. They could get the idea that she is not experiencing proper social development. But Talia has friends. After all, she is a member of the human race which is characteristically social. She needs parents and peers just like anybody else. Remember she is the one who jumped out of the car to be with Colleen and Heather.

Yet Talia has some preferences which make her much different than Jimmy. She tends to relate to friends in group settings rather than one-on-one situations. She spends considerable time working on projects by herself. She enjoys

Children have basic distinctions:
- **In how they relate to people**
- **In the way they learn**
- **In what excites them**
- **In the kind of discipline they need**

filling out her workbook by doing exercise after exercise on her own, emerging only when she needs some help. She focused on making her toy kitchen neat and creating order in her dresser drawer.

Notice how Talia makes decisions to focus only on one thing and to deal thoroughly with that single issue. Her parents should note, as they observe her over the years, that she might not do well trying to keep a number of balls in the air. Given the basement and messy room stories, she appears to be quite able to look at a large amount of disorder and make a decision about where she should direct her attention. She doesn't allow unaccomplished tasks to disturb the precision with which she completes what she wants to do. When Talia gets to high school, she will probably demonstrate proficiency in doing independent assignments.

In contrast, certain teachers are likely to have mild dissatisfaction that Jimmy "hasn't matured enough to work on his own." But the coaches and science teachers will think differently. They will perceive him as an outstanding leader, always involving his team members and lab partners.

After considering the contrasts between Talia and Jimmy, you may be able by now to figure out why Jimmy didn't do his homework. Are you ready to venture a guess at this point? Do you have any ideas? Here are the actual facts.

Dad was away on a business trip, which soured Jimmy's attitude. He was used to spending some quality time with his father every day. Mom was so busy with Dad gone, she had no time to spend working with Jimmy. Instead, she just told him to make sure he did his schoolwork. Since he had never missed doing his homework before, she didn't think to check it. When it was discovered that he wasn't doing his assignments, Jimmy's mom and his teachers became concerned. He still felt resentment over being somewhat ignored, so he exploited the situation. And

An answer at last: Why didn't Jimmy do his homework?

as the concern over Jimmy increased, so did his self-pity and stubbornness.

So how did the adults in Jimmy's life finally convince him to start doing his homework again? Well, since the parents knew something of Jimmy's design, they didn't need to convince him. Rather, the whole problem dissolved when Dad came home, didn't say a word about homework, and told Jimmy how much he missed him. They sat down together after dinner (as usual), and Dad worked while Jimmy caught up on his assignments. About halfway through this session, the following conversation took place:

"Jimmy, I understand there was a little problem about your homework."

With a *"Yes, Dad,"* the story was told in a subdued voice.

"Well, Jimmy, I must say it makes me feel good to know that you miss me while I'm gone."

"I do, but what's that got to do with homework?"

"It all wouldn't have happened if I hadn't left and you hadn't reacted to my leaving."

"I guess that's true."

"But there's something you need to understand. That good dinner we had tonight is the result of my working and earning the money to pay for it. My job requires me to take trips to other cities once in a while. Though I enjoy traveling, I don't enjoy being away from my family, including you, of course. But that's my job and you need to help me do my job like I help you with your job."

"I don't have a job."

"Being a student and doing your homework is your job. When you fall down on your job, you make things hard for everybody—your mom, your teachers, and especially me. I need to be able to count on you when I'm away."

"But Mom wouldn't help me!"

"Jimmy, the truth is that she was too busy with me

In college, it will make sense for Jimmy to seek a study group to work with or to set up one of his own. It would be foolish in this case to treat Jimmy's God-given design as an idiosyncrasy he will grow out of. It is actually a strength and could be a feature of how he will operate in a career.

gone, and you don't like to work by yourself. But there are times when things won't work out the way you like them to, and you are going to have to work alone. That's the way it's going to be at times. When those times come, I would like to be able to depend on you."

"But I hate doing homework alone."

"Are you serious! You hate to do *anything* alone. I guess that's how God made you, which is fine with me because that's you. So someday when you have a job, you will probably want one where you work with other people. But this world is not perfect. There will be times when you have to do things by yourself and you want to be able to do good work. This homework business was one of those times and you didn't do a good job, so I'm afraid some discipline is in order. Does that make sense?"

"Yeah, I guess so."

Jimmy's parents have followed up this discussion by including certain solo tasks into his daily schedule. But they can't expect that Jimmy will eventually love to work alone. (At some point in parent training school, a misled authority taught all parents the odd idea that hated tasks become loved if repeated enough.)

CONSISTENCIES AND RECURRING THEMES

Talia, meanwhile, finds it preferable to work on her own. She displays organizational skills, and works with precision. She probably could be asked to do more exacting work than would be normally expected for a girl her age. It's still a little early to tell whether her interest in the number of friends orbiting around her is a social requirement. Perhaps she is simply inclined to work "on" instead of "with" people. A more sophisticated adult who displays what Talia may be evidencing would be capable of working with precision teams in business or industry. That possibility need not be decided for Talia now, but it serves as an example of how acorns grow into mighty oaks.

An isolated incident or two may not let you know anything for sure about your child's design, but they will help you look for a consistent pattern as the child continues to grow.

If our suspicions are confirmed, the listening that goes on in the classroom is a very important resource for Talia's educational growth.

Another possible discovery about Talia is the frequency with which she inserts herself into other families at the shopping mall (a curious habit for a nonteam person). This adds credence to her potential interest in people, for what ends we don't yet know. But the outstanding fact is that she is fascinated with what is being said between people. It opens up the possibility that listening is an important means for her to learn. Again, we cannot draw strong conclusions, but it certainly is a nugget to store away for future confirmation.

Talia's love for listening to others certainly goes along with her interest in group situations rather than one-on-one. In the latter situation she has to spend half her time listening and the other half talking. But in a group situation, she could spend all of her time listening and learning—probably adding enough of her own contributions to be responsible. In a group, the amount of talk any one person has to do is reduced.

Meanwhile, Jimmy's concern at the shopping mall is with saving money and acquiring something. When Jimmy finds a sale, he thinks in terms of a double acquisition—he gets both the item he purchases and the money that is saved. What he might buy is probably not as important to him as the deal he makes. His parents wisely remember the pile of paper airplanes which were not played with. The planes were fine since Jimmy manufactured them out of available paper, but other collections can be costly and rather useless. Traditional collections such as insects, minerals, stamps, books, or coins are worth encouraging if he shows interest, because they provide both value and an accompanying body of knowledge.

Jimmy's parents are careful that he acquire items which not only satisfy his acquisitional interest but also provide good play experiences.

While Jimmy and Talia are bouncing up and down basement stairs and in and out of cars, little Megan was slipped in as a tiny contrast to her brother and sister. As she plays with her dolls, we are not going to even suggest that this is the first indicator of a particular career. But we must keep in mind that the first evidence *could* start this early.

We will rejoice that whether she is displaying a natural interest for a girl in that phase of development, or whether she is beginning in miniature that which may become a major expression in life, we know she is not like any other person.

In our professional roles we have observed and identified the operating style of innumerable individuals. Such observations allow us to note the behavior of children with great confidence that there is meaning to what they do. Yet we don't want to attribute more or less value to these observations than they deserve.

It is one thing to accurately describe consistencies over many years in the way adults act in given situations. It is another to evaluate children with their confusion of motives, needs, and developmental factors. But in our experience, most children display plenty of fresh evidence about the particular ways they go about doing what they do. It makes sense for parents to take this rich resource into account. It will both enhance their parenting and prevent them from putting their children into boxes from which they are never allowed to escape.

Though Megan has the same parents as those of Talia and Jimmy, the same values, the same everything, she turns out different. Isn't that the genius of God?

TOOLS FOR YOUR USE

W hat geniuses we would be if we could handle all problems with children in real life as smoothly as we can in a book! Any parent knows instinctively that "it ain't all that easy." But our roles as parents will become somewhat more effective if we don't lose sight of a very important fact. We must remember that Jimmy's hidden world was closed to us until we were willing to look behind his outward actions and see him as God made him.

We must see that God designed a unique personality and not an undefined hunk of clay to be shaped into what man wants. Jimmy already has a design and we must nurture what is already there. And what is true about Jimmy is true about your children as well. *Each child is designed, and you can know something of that design.*

All of us learn early in life that other people have expectations of who we are supposed to be. Parents,

We must give up the idea of seeing children through rose-tinted glasses of:
- **What we want them to be**
- **What society expects of them**
- **Our measuring sticks**
- **Our categories, boxes, classifications, and groupings**

We make a lot of effort to conform to other people's expectations, sometimes to our benefit and other times to our detriment.

friends, teachers, brothers and sisters, playmates, class-mates, and relatives all take part in trying to shape us—whether intentionally or unintentionally. As kids, our peers expected us to behave in ways that our parents could not approve of. Our teachers and parents had expectations which weren't always consistent with one another. One teacher expected unthinking obedience while another challenged us not to respond without thinking through what we are being obedient to. One parent expected mannerly responsiveness, the other aggressive competitiveness.

Given the mix of expectations, it is no wonder so few people grow up with any understanding of who they are, except in the most general terms. It certainly explains why many adults have little idea what to do with their lives. We have only a vague idea of what uniqueness we bring to the world of work, and no understanding of our calling.

In view of this confusion, it is a delight to find some order in human behavior, as we did when we focused on Jimmy. There we were able to discover enough of his design to solve an irritating problem. To keep things simple, we selected just a few items as examples of what to look for. When we look at the *total* behavior of Jimmy, or of any person, it becomes complicated to discover any kind of order. Only foolish people feel confident with a simple analysis of what is going on in any situation.

People do many things for many reasons, and trying to understand why can be very frustrating.

Family life adds another dimension to the confusion of this process of understanding one another. Both parents and children are capable of subterfuge in their relationships. If not careful, they can easily end up with stupefyingly complex scenarios, some of which look uncomfortably like TV soap operas.

FOUR CATEGORIES OF BEHAVIOR

To help you cut through the confusion without getting an advanced degree in human behavior, we suggest thinking in terms of four major categories of behavior. Remember these groupings are to organize behavior, not to explain it. (All four categories of behavior are seen in everyone except infants.)

GROUP #1—Utilitarian Actions

Most things people do every day are activities which are practical and necessary. Cleaning house, doing the laundry, repairing a carburetor, learning to add and subtract, fixing breakfast, putting toys away, mowing the lawn, attending a committee meeting, building a fence, and performing your duties at work are all examples of activities which have to be done whether or not the individual likes it. Necessity characterizes these actions. (More will be said about this kind of behavior in Chapters 14, 15, and 16.)

GROUP #2—Developmental Actions

A number of people's activities are for their own development, whether those activities are voluntary or mandatory. Jogging, doing homework, skateboarding, prayer, lifting weights, memorizing birdcalls, Bible study, learning Spanish, studying history, practicing pitching, and dieting are all examples. These activities may or may not have any practical value outside their effect on the individual doing them, but they improve or expand the person's capabilities. (Chapters 17, 18, 19, and 20 will go into greater detail about how your child develops.)

GROUP #3—Relational Actions

Some activities seem to be utilitarian and may indeed accomplish something practical, yet the basic reason for the action is relational. The individual acts in order to please another or to make an impact on someone. The degree of involvement in the activity is determined by the degree of response desired.

Jill cleans up the kitchen not because she hates a mess. One look at her room will make that clear. She takes care of the kitchen because Mom will be pleased when she comes home. And once in a while Jill wants Mom to know that she cares.

Lyle plays football with Dad on Saturday mornings. Why? Because Dad loves football. Dad talks football, eats in front of the TV when a game is on, reads football magazines, and keeps up with all the teams. He gave Lyle a football at the ripe old age of three weeks. Sure, he has lots of fun playing, but his primary motivation is to please Dad. Years later Lyle will abandon football (in which he will have developed considerable skill) in favor of tennis. His father won't understand the reasons, but Lyle will be choosing a sport based on his own inclinations which are more individualistic.

Lyle is no dummy. He knows the way to Dad's heart is through football.

Both Jill and Lyle were involved with activities which are *indirectly* relational in nature. Other actions are *directly* relational. It is obvious that such actions take place because of the feelings one person has for another. Kissing, shaking hands, hugging, sending flowers, and giving gifts are all actions which are by nature designed to express personal feelings. Kicking, hitting, punching, and similar actions may be less desirable, but are still in the category of direct relational actions. (Look for more about this kind of behavior in Chapter 21.)

GROUP #4—Expressive Actions

An expressive action emerges from the heart of an individual. There are two kinds of such actions. The first is *play activity*, which can include sports, recreation, amusement, or spontaneous expression. Examples include playing games, singing, fishing, building sand castles, flying kites, soccer, praiseful worship, skipping, sculpting, rolling down hills, skiing, chewing bubble gum, writing poetry, whistling, and drawing pictures.

Expressive actions are those things you *like* to do.

A second type of expressive actions are *psychogenic activities*. These are compulsive actions which are prompted by internal emotional conflicts. Hurting someone, shouting and swearing, deliberately breaking toys, breaking dishes against the wall, destroying relationships, and breaking up families are examples. (Expressive behavior is further examined in Chapter 22.)

Since the previous four categories reflect the nature of a human being, almost any action we take will fall into one of the groupings. You and I have a desire to survive, so we do utilitarian things to ensure cleanliness, comfort, and order for ourselves and others. God created us as social beings, so we need to establish relationships with others and feel loved. We are created with a potential for spiritual, physical, emotional, and intellectual growth, so we develop ourselves. And finally, God made us a playful and imaginative race, so we act accordingly. These four families of behavior are universal to mankind.

While it is true that each of us shares behavior common to all people, it is also true that something about each individual is unique.

WHERE IS THE UNIQUENESS?

We attempt to identify one another's uniqueness in the way we make comments about people. The phrases we use are familiar:

Jim's a good pitcher.

Mary's an excellent gardener.

She's such a good child.

Ken is so humorless.

Joe is a preppie dresser.

June is certainly disorganized.

We observe a repeated fragment of someone's behavior and then make generalizations. There is nothing wrong with this practice as long as our generalizations are true. It

We too often make hasty generalizations based on limited observations.

is a common method of evaluation, but it stops short. We treat the generalization as a label which we assume in some way captures the *essence* of an individual. But a little thoughtful reflection will quickly reveal how narrow-minded that assumption is.

Hidden behind all the actions which we have so neatly organized into four categories is a powerful core—what biblically is called the heart. But the heart is not a vague spiritual capacity tucked somewhere within us. It is the foundation of human personality from which *all* actions emerge. This heart has a shape, a design which can be described. In an adult it can be described in great detail. In your child it can be described in enough detail to transform your understanding of who he or she is.

Isn't it wonderful to know that your son or daughter, even after only a few years of life, is not just a blob of personality that is slowly and somewhat haphazardly gathering its form?

How glorious to realize that children are designed like jewels that bear the beauty God intended from the very beginning of their creation. So does that mean we already have little doctors, plumbers, mathematicians, cabinet makers, and artists running around in our houses? Does that mean all we have to do now is feed and water these diminutive professionals to have them automatically turn out to be whatever is already fixed in their makeup?

The answer is that God does not create doctors and plumbers. Rather, He creates individuals who possess the gifts to become a doctor or a plumber. We, in turn, need to equip ourselves by acquiring the education and training necessary to become proficient in our designed areas. We are required to develop skills and acquire knowledge to match our gifts. Only after people have applied their God-given gifts toward their designed professions is it right to conclude that God has indeed given us those doctors and plumbers.

When someone attempts to accomplish work for which they have no gifts, they disturb the intended balance that God has established.

With this in mind, let us look at your child. If you have more than one child, keep in mind that each one is designed in a unique way. In this sinful world, we cannot actually see the designs of our children. Sometime, in a future kingdom, our spiritual sight will be restored. Then, as we look at our children as God designed them, we will be stunned to see what wondrous creations were running around our houses. Meanwhile, we do not have to proceed entirely by faith in this matter. There is much that you as a parent can do to be better informed about your child's design while you have the opportunity.

PERCEIVING YOUR CHILD'S DESIGN

Evidence for your child's design is all about you. It appears in the four categories of activities described previously. Yet to discover specific elements of your child's design, you must look beyond the categorized behaviors to perceive the person behind the actions. The categories are helpful in understanding what response you may need to provide in a given situation, but the real child begins to appear when you are able to get behind their actions to discover a common theme—what we will call their *motif*.

It will be enormously helpful if you are careful at this point to see the word *motif* as a door to understanding the nature of your child as well as your own nature. Walk through that door—even if word studies leave you cold. We are dealing with more than a concept; we are dealing with your child. If you have the wrong ideas about that child, that misinformation can be dangerous.

To dramatize the importance of proper understanding, just consider the distorted ideas many people have about the human fetus which have led to an incredibly high number of abortions. Contrast the difference between thinking that a child is a temporary biochemical process with believing that a child is a creation of God with an eternal destiny.

Words and the ideas they represent are important. The kind of parenting we do and the children we welcome into the world are profoundly affected by the mental concepts we adhere to. So a close examination of the concept of *motif* is in order at this point.

motif *n* **1** Recurring salient thematic element in a work of art; a dominant idea or central theme; a repeated design; **2** an influence or stimulus prompting to action.

A motif is a recurring salient element in a work of art. The first fact we discover here is that your child is a work of art. Physical appearance may or may not indicate outer beauty, but that is not especially important. Our real appearances are seen by God since He looks on the heart. Each child is created beautiful by God—no matter what may ultimately happen to both exterior and inner beauty. Your child's beauty also has a salient element (a striking theme or an outstanding characteristic). This is further established by the next phrase of the definition.

A motif is a dominant idea or central theme. Your child is unique, like no other. His or her prominent qualities can be described and woven together to make up the essential characteristics (theme) of his or her life. These dominant qualities are authored by God. They embrace all the physical, emotional, spiritual, and psychological dimensions of our being.

A motif is a repeated design, an influence or stimulus prompting to action. Your child's design is not just a shape somewhere in the interior of the personality, but rather a motivation to action. It involves the heart, from which all actions emerge. The heart is the place of the will, the seat of all intentionality. And design is tied to intentionality. There is consistency to all that your child does. Your child does certain things in certain ways that are unlike any other child. That is why Jimmy and Talia and Megan were so different, even though they came from the same household.

The four categories of your child's actions (utilitarian, relational, developmental, and expressive) make possible a wide variety of behavior. But if you really want to see some of the God-given design of your child, you need to find a repeated theme that influences all of your child's actions and decisions.

We saw some of this in Jimmy. The consistency of his behavior revealed exactly how he learns and goes about doing his homework assignments. As a result, his parents

> It is He who made us, and we are His (Psalm 100:3).

> Look for a repeated, consistent theme that permeates your child's likes or dislikes in whatever he or she does.

could make very specific responses to him. What a difference knowing the right facts can make!

APPRECIATING CONSISTENCY

The importance of attributing value to consistent behavior is not new. When a child is emotionally or physically ill, we are aware of the need to analyze patterns of aberrant behavior in order to develop a strategy for healing. Career counselors understand that consistency is a valuable tool for assisting people in evaluating their skills. Even youngsters choosing players for their teams make decisions based on previous consistent athletic performance.

Our lack of attention to consistent behavior becomes evident, however, in the context of all the normal activities of daily life—at home, on the job, and in leisure activities. There we assume that management training can produce managers, and that a one-formula-fits-all approach can transform nonmanagers into effective leaders. We believe that majoring in education in college will make us teachers, in spite of overwhelming evidence to the contrary. (Most of us come up with a very short list of teachers who really made a difference in our lives, and a much longer list of teachers who had the credentials but not the gift.)

You can expect to see a consistency in your child's way of operating—in accomplishing chores, organizing toys, responding to stories, entertaining himself, embracing or ignoring peers, being attracted to certain kinds of toys, fascination with certain kinds of objects, competitive spirit, response to confusion, orderliness, choice of playthings on a trip, sports interests, and what he collects. His or her life is a rich display of uniqueness. A reasonable knowledge of such uniqueness can delight you as parent and equip you for excellence in your role.

The world has taught us that we are always developing, which is true. But we have also been told that we can become anything we want to become, which isn't true.

A Slightly FEISTY Dialogue

In this chapter we have tried to anticipate your response to many of the things we have been saying so far. We are presenting an imaginary dialogue between you, the readers, and us, the authors. We hope we include any questions you may want to raise. You begin the conversation.

The categories you provided in the last chapter are helpful. I can go along with people being utilitarian, relational, developmental, or expressive. But do you think people are always that neat in their behavior?

No, not always. People often have more than one reason behind any action they take. But analysis is easier when we use categories of one kind or other.

So you don't insist on your set of categories?

Certainly not. Professionals who study people's behavior probably have other categories which they would prefer using. However, we feel we need to distance ourselves to some degree from terminology and categories relating to the pathological concerns of psychiatry.

What's the difference?

The emphasis there is on what is wrong with people. But this book is not dealing with what is wrong with our children. As we identify their operating styles, we must look at them positively.

Your approach to child rearing is beginning to sound sentimentally optimistic.

Well, sometimes Christians are in danger of sounding so, but they can be optimistic for good reason. In this case, we base our conclusions on logic. You cannot identify an individual's strengths by concentrating on negatives. So as you observe your child, you have to sift through behavior and extract significant positive evidence that can help you identify the way God designed him or her.

Are you suggesting that the traditional academic methods developed in our universities for understanding human behavior are somehow suspect?

Often the universities develop methods that lead to wonderful advances in human progress. But remember that all such institutions are made up of human beings who are fallible. On a grand scale, we can put satellites in orbit around distant planets and perform organ transplants. Yet we can't seem to guide our addled adolescents into reasonable career paths. In our schools we still cram students of all ages and backgrounds into learning situations while we barely recognize how and why they learn.

Are you suggesting that there have been no advances in learning theory?

It depends on which specific area you are referring to. There have been advances in educational techniques. We've also done better in understanding the connection between the developmental phases of learning and a child's level of maturity. So educators now know, for example, at what age a child is likely to begin understanding

If we had focused only on Jimmy's negative behavior, we may never have discovered the root of his problem.

abstractions. But some researchers in the field of people behavior will flatly state that even after twenty-five years of rigorous study, we still have had no significant advances in understanding *how* people learn—in spite of the millions of dollars poured into research on the subject.

Those are some strong statements.

Yes they are, but they need to be made. Even if this viewpoint turns out to represent the malcontent critics in the field, we could reduce the statistics by half and we still wouldn't paint an encouraging picture.

How do you explain the slow rate of growth in the area of learning, especially when recent research has turned up so many new discoveries on the body and the brain?

It is easier to probe and observe physical, tangible things than it is to comprehend the much more complex terrain of the human spirit. In addition, researchers have tended to focus on the presence or absence of a particular kind of intelligence that can be apprehended by IQ testing. A child with a high IQ is perceived to be a quick learner. A lower IQ clues researchers that a child won't learn efficiently. But what if there are different kinds of intelligences? Who's to say that there aren't many ways that people learn?

Why are we so successful in our research on the physiological functions of the body, but so sluggish in gathering relevant information about learning?

Dominant theories explaining human behavior usually have been derived by studying groups of people instead of individuals, and by extracting generalizations from the data. These are then translated into models to which our institutions pressure people to imitate. In this way, universities have almost always seen the individual as if he were raw material to be molded into whatever society needs. Educational institutions can be big on conformity.

What if a unique pattern of learning is an inherent part of every person's personality?

In contrast, the biblical view is that each human is an individual. When that individuality is taken into account, the person can be effectively nurtured and developed.

But aren't Jews and Christians especially guilty of trying to make their kids conform to rules and regulations?

There are different kinds of gifts (I Corinthians 12:4).

Think of yourself with sober judgment, in accordance with the measure of faith God has given you (Romans 12:3).

To each one of us grace has been given as Christ apportioned it (Ephesians 4:7).

Don't they talk about wanting their kids to learn how to yield to God's will? That sounds like conformity to me.

True. Parents who believe in God know that their children need to learn early that there is an ultimate authority to whom they are responsible. For centuries, Jews and Christians have passed that understanding on from generation to generation. But it is also true that Christians and Jews have been taught that each of us have been given differing gifts. Accordingly, we are likely to exhibit different behavior under the same circumstances.

So even with the necessity of a certain amount of conforming behavior, you're saying that children have different patterns of behavior emerging from different gifts and different measures of God-given faith . . . as well as different psychological backgrounds, different cultures, and differing personalities. And all these differences affirm the need of the four categories you provided for us to use. Correct?

Correct. Just don't lose sight of your original observation. The fact that we've identified four neat categories does not mean that your child's behavior will be limited to one category at a time. Categories can be mixed. In the last chapter, Lyle was described as playing football primarily to please his father—relational behavior. In another scenario, the same action might have been an opportunity to develop himself physically—a developmental motive. Or he might have described getting rid of his frustration with one of the players by tackling him at every opportunity—an expressive purpose.

None of these reasons would justify encouraging Lyle to continue football if the sport weren't fun for him. That's why he later found tennis to be better at allowing him to express his natural interests in individual performance and athletic form. His decision came after a healthy relationship with his father (which football had helped to develop) enabled Lyle to make independent decisions.

I'm ready to move on now. Before I do, would you like to summarize what you've told me in a couple of closing sentences?

At the hub of all the diversity in human behavior you can discover the consistency of God-given individual operating styles which can be observed and described. And you can take comfort in the fact that you *can* make sense out of your child's behavior.

There are logically explained reasons behind all human behavior, though all human behavior is not logical.

GATHERING THE Evidence

Your child is a distinct, unique creation of God. Obviously, he looks different than all his friends. Even though there may be strong family resemblances, he can be picked out from among the rest of his relatives. He will probably learn at a faster or slower pace than his brothers, sisters, and peers. These are all distinctions that are apparent, but we need to go much farther in recognizing a child's uniqueness.

We have warned that the world will attempt to cram your child into molds devised by those who have little appreciation of a biblical view of man. It is our goal to help you equip your child to not only dodge those molds, but also to enjoy what God has done in his life by creating him to be distinct.

God does not call Christians to a higher plane of living without giving them the means to get there. In this case, the means has little to do with what your child looks like or how rapidly he learns. Rather, the key to discovering your child's design is in your vision. We want to help you see your child's behavior and be able to envision the essence of what God has created.

Before we describe the specific techniques in the process of discovering your child's design, we recommend that you consider what degree of detail you need for your situation. If your child is very young, a few major elements may be enough to be quite useful. For an older adolescent, much detail may be required for purposes of career and educational planning.

BENEFITS OF DISCOVERING YOUR CHILD'S DESIGN

As your child goes through each phase of development, different benefits of knowing his design will become apparent to you. Several of these benefits are listed below in somewhat of a developmental sequence. As you read through them, keep in mind that each of the benefits is true at all times. But depending on the age of your child at a given point, one or more of them may be especially relevant.

Development Can Be Enhanced—The rate of development for children is uneven. A ten year old may seem to have equilibrium, with no serious concerns to disturb his easygoing life. Then the eleventh year comes with all kinds of problems in his relationships with parents and peers. How can this kid who gracefully negotiated a problem-free life suddenly turn into a complex, self-critical eleven year old?

Whenever a child encounters a confusing year, it helps for the parent to provide some realistic evidence of his or her dependable consistencies.

Knowing how the child operates can help parents reduce his conflict to a reasonable degree—if there *is* such a thing as a reasonable degree. The internal clashes which have him confused cannot be eliminated, but it helps to have parents who can quietly affirm (out of consistent experience) just who this eleven year old is.

Child: *"I can't do anything right!"*
Parent: "I sometimes feel that way myself, but I would
guess that isn't entirely true about you."
Child: *"What d'ya mean?"*
Parent: "I don't know anyone in our family who is as
organized (or caring, patient, etc.) as you."
(Appropriate examples should be given.)

Uniqueness Can Be Affirmed—With their young lives being frequently bombarded by the media, children can become too aware of what fragments of humanity they are. It is important that they are initiated as quickly as possible into an awareness of their uniqueness. In the beginning it is enough for them to be unique to Mom and Dad. Once they are aware of the outside world, however, they increasingly need evidence that their parents' opinions are based on more than sentiment. Such evidence should come through hundreds of conversations, through personal experience, and through being taught how to look at one's life.

Individuality Can Be Appreciated—It is important to hold fast to the knowledge that each person is of value. Holocausts, world wars, and terrorist action have left all of us with a need for assurance that we have worth as individuals. Such affirmation does not come so much through formal means as through strong relationships. We should make special effort to relate to our children in a way which will reinforce each individual's worth and dignity while we also make them aware of other people's value.

Appropriate Play Opportunities Can Be Cultivated—Play is not primarily for the purpose of keeping children busy till they grow up. It is the child's arena for development. Some development involves motor skills, and is as universal as learning how to crawl before walking. Other play activities provide a child with ways to express his or her uniqueness. What one child plays with, another finds uninteresting. One child will line up dolls and animals for school while another is more involved with their wardrobe.

A child who likes to build will begin with blocks, but will eventually need more sophisticated building toys as his stage of skill development can handle it. If you don't supply toys with which to make bridges, don't be surprised if your books are used as a substitute—and don't be too hard on the child for doing so.

A Fitting Social Style Can Be Encouraged—We all need to interact with other people in order to become a whole person. In addition to the family style of relating to people, most children will operate in relationship to others according to the way they are designed by God. Some children are gregarious, and some let others initiate friendships. In encouraging your child's social development, consider his or her style and not yours. One child leaves the house and gets involved with the neighborhood kids. Another heads right for the sandbox to play by himself. Both are fine if that is really where they enjoy being. A few years later, perhaps some teacher will note that your sandbox child does not socialize enough. Unless we are talking about extreme behavior, one should not worry or try to change the pattern of behavior. Just wait and see. In a few years another teacher will note that the same child shows a mature ability to work independently.

Formal Learning Can Be Facilitated—This benefit is important enough to justify its own chapter later in the book. At this point it is enough to realize that each child learns in a different way and for different reasons. Some learn for the sake of learning. Some learn in order to apply the knowledge to a particular situation. Others have little intrinsic interest in learning, yet can be motivated with a fitting payoff of one kind or another. Your child's learning style is obviously an important element of his design.

Problem Solving Can Be Enhanced—As the child matures, he or she encounters a variety of normal problems at home and in school. Some children thrive on these situations. Others don't. When problem solving is not a major strength for a child, the parent can become a compensating ally. You complement the child's weakness with your strength, or you suggest someone else who has the appropriate gifts. This system works all the better if the parent will occasionally request help from the child when the tables are turned. Sometimes the child can compensate

One of the consistent requirements of becoming an adult is the increasing demand to solve problems—from learning to tie one's shoes to understanding the meaning of life.

with his or her skill in an area when the parent is willing to ask.

Establishing such a give-and-take relationship with your child will demonstrate that everyone has strengths and weaknesses. An important function of parenting is enabling your offspring to use his or her strengths to develop a useful strategy in handling problems. And the transition of responsibility from parent to child also helps the child discover and become comfortable with his own design.

Effective Career Counseling and Education Can Be Provided—Toward the end of the junior year in high school, a strategy for developing some general career goals should be developed between parent and child. This strategy should be followed by a discussion of the kind of education necessary to bring those goals into reality. The operating style and unique strengths of the student should be compared to specific careers, especially in terms of the tasks and activities involved for each potential vocation.

HOW DO YOU LEARN?

Now that we've covered several of the benefits of discovering your child's design, let's move into the area of how learning takes place. As we do so, we are going to shift the focus from your child to yourself—at least, for a while.

After you determine how much detail you need in observing your child's behavior, it's time to learn the necessary techniques. As you begin to learn these techniques, you are likely to realize something of your own design. You probably prefer to learn in a particular way. Since this information is appearing in book form, it may or may not fit your learning style. Perhaps you would have preferred to hear the information on an audiocassette or to see it presented visually on a video. If so, you are likely to adapt the *actual* method of teaching to your *desired* method. You might wait for another format, or perhaps have a spouse read the book and then tell you what it's all about.

Adults accept teaching methods as they come, even if those methods aren't geared to their strengths. Children may need help with this process.

And after you learn the information, your design will also determine how you apply it. Sometimes this process needs adaptation as well. For example, after reading this material you might throw yourself into the process and keep at it until you've mastered it. Or you might go strong for a while, pause for a bit, and then pick it up again—short-term accelerations rather than long-term continuity. Or you might wait until a problem strikes to apply the information at all.

At this point, take some time to reflect and characterize how you are likely to go about learning something. In each case, be as specific as possible.

Take a few moments to answer some key questions.

(1) How do you learn?

(2) Provide some examples to justify your conclusion about how you learn. (Use both recent and past examples.)

(3) Once you learn something, characterize how you usually go about applying it. (Only when there is a problem? On a continuing basis? In long-term application? In spurts of activity, as needed? Until you have thoroughly mastered it?)

(4) How might your style of learning naturally help you discover your child's design? How might your own learning style interfere with discovering your child's design?

TECHNIQUES FOR GATHERING EVIDENCE

Two major techniques are helpful in gathering the evidence of your child's design. The first is observation, where you watch your child's behavior and record what you see. The second is story telling, where you encourage your child to talk about activities he or she liked doing. Both of these techniques will warrant a chapter of their own, but we will introduce the concepts at this point.

Observation

The younger the child, the more you will need to depend on observation as a method of gathering data. Infants obviously can't respond to your urging for them to share information, so you are restricted to the evidence you can gather through observation alone. Yet observation remains an important technique in the life of the older child, too, where you have the advantage of being able to confirm what you are told by what you have witnessed.

As you begin to make observations regarding a child, do so without forming any conclusions at first. Later, after you have gone through some analysis of your child's design, you will be able to put your observations into a proper perspective. At that point you will need to carefully continue to identify new information and not get locked into previous patterns of behavior.

At all times, first assume that any pattern of behavior is expressive of the child's design rather than a budding neurosis of some kind. We are not suggesting that your child is incapable of producing negative behavior, but even when producing such behavior he or she will probably express it in a particular style. One child will be disobedient in one way, and his sister in another. In both cases the behavior is undesirable, yet reveals something different about the strengths of the child.

The categories of behavior provided in Chapter 5 (utilitarian, relational, developmental, and expressive) embrace

Your child's design can be recognized even in his or her negative behavior.

almost all possible reasons behind a person's actions. Each category is a stage upon which your child makes certain kinds of moves which you observe. You should train yourself to have the detachment of a journalist who is getting the facts of the story and nothing but the facts. This is not always easy because *you* are often one of the actors on stage with your child. In your role, it is natural for you to become emotionally involved due to your strong feelings about what is happening. Sometimes, however, it is important to separate your parental functions from your journalistic one.

A defiant child who has just dumped his bowl of oatmeal all over the floor is going to test the objectivity of any parent on the receiving end of this action. In fact, at that point the temptation is to apply standard procedure and forget about any kind of detachment. But at other times, you will be able to maintain your objectivity and gather much useful information about your child.

Your role as objective journalist will sometimes (by necessity) succumb to your need to be a vivid, involved character in your child's life.

Story Telling

Another way of getting evidence is to ask for it! For example, when Jimmy and Talia were asked what they liked about doing their workbooks, one expressed an interest in the *process* of doing it ("I like doing it.") The other made it clear that *completing* it is important ("I like finishing it.") Though such comments in isolation do not contribute much, when supported by enough other examples and observations they become precise expressions of each child's design.

Much of what people say is in response to the expectations of others given the particular circumstances. For example, if you are walking down the street and meet an acquaintance who asks how you are, you might very possibly reply, "Fine," even if you have a throbbing headache. Why? Because you are not expected to give a fact-filled health report. The inquiry was merely a greeting.

We are expected to follow certain "scripts" in work, school, and church settings as well. Though the style in which we respond may vary, we usually have little opportunity to honestly express ourselves. Therefore, when people are presented with an opportunity to talk about activities which are meaningful to them, they reveal much about whom God designed them to be. Even very shy people have little difficulty in telling their stories, because they know them so well.

The next two chapters will take you farther in the development of the techniques of observation and storytelling. Examples will be provided so you can see how they work. And you'll get involved with each of these methods and experience the benefits they provide for any parent who really wants to discover his or her child's design.

When given the opportunity to talk about themselves, most people experience pleasure in expressing the facts of their own special nature.

MAKING OBSERVATIONS

Parents are in a highly strategic position when it comes to gathering evidence for their child's design. No one else has the opportunity to observe the child's actions in so many conditions and situations. This fact seems rather obvious, but is worth mentioning here. Parents play a supervisory role so often that they occasionally fail to see all the drama taking place about them.

Even when doing ordinary things, a person's actions express something of the unique individual he or she happens to be. Merely walking down the hall displays a distinctive expression.

How much more revealing are the complex activities of play and school when discovering a child's design. Careful observation of these activities will reveal splendid consistencies. To aid in the process, we recommend keeping a journal.

You can sharpen your observations as you pay special attention to: (1) Activities which your child likes doing, and (2) Activities where the child has the freedom to choose how to do something.

BEGINNING A DESIGN JOURNAL

We refer to such a journal as a Design Journal. And as you start to keep your Design Journal, you will soon discover that it will help you record several valuable pieces of information.

(1) *Record the action.* A primary purpose of your journal is to record your child's actions. This is where you imagine yourself as an objective reporter, gathering only facts. At this early stage you should be totally disinterested in anybody's opinion about those facts, including your own. All you want to include in this section of the Design Journal are notes describing specific actions. You need only make a record of them, taking notes on both primary and secondary actions.

You need not look for anything exotic to record. A wealth of material is all about you.

Primary actions include specific accomplishments. For example: a building of blocks was put together, a jigsaw puzzle was assembled, a bath drain was unplugged, a drawing was completed, a tricycle or bicycle was ridden for the first time, a school project was finished, a toy battle was fought, seeds were planted, bread was baked, a room was organized, a club was established, a collection was assembled, a playpen was outgrown, costumes were made, scrapbooks were put together, races were run, picnics were organized, etc.

Secondary actions are the activities that either precede or follow the primary actions. For instance: all the necessary tools were gathered, someone was persuaded to join the team, a mess was cleaned up, directions were read and followed, shapes were analyzed, materials were located and assembled, practice took place, something was designed on paper, a procedure was learned, information was obtained, words were mastered, skills were learned, a team was formed, an animal was trained, paint was applied, ingredients were weighed, a process was controlled, a script was followed, a fantasy was created, a list was made, and so forth.

(2) Record significant quotes from your observation. As your child is involved in his or her activities, you will overhear a running commentary. The second function of the Design Journal is to record useful quotes, such as: "It's more fun when Bobby plays with me," "I like drawings that are hard to do," "My tower is higher than yours," "Do it like the picture says," "Let me change it," "There are too many pieces," "I like math," "Now let me tell you a scary story," "Can I help you make the cookies?" "Show me how," "I'm the teacher," "Let's do a different one," "I hate baseball," "Do it right!" or "Let's see where we end up."

(3) Record significant quotes gleaned from the child's story telling. You may not happen to overhear enough to let you know clearly what the child is thinking or feeling. So as you question him a bit, record his responses in this third section of the Design Journal. This process is described in detail in the next chapter.

(4) Record your preliminary ideas about what you see. As you gather and record observations, you will start to see the emergence of certain themes or consistencies. You might discover that your child doesn't like to make a move until he knows exactly what is expected, likes to organize his room and his toys even when they don't need it, likes to do things with others, likes to write stories, doesn't like to read instructions, or so forth. You should write down these consistencies whether they are fully proven facts or mere suspicions. As they accumulate in your Design Journal, they become a major resource for reaching some clear conclusions about your child.

If you have more than one child, it is best to keep separate Design Journals for each one. You should at least keep clearly separated sections in the Design Journal so your observations don't get mixed up.

LEARNING TO ACCEPT WHAT GOD HAS DONE

Having worked with many parents over the years, we realize a too common tendency among many of them. Some encourage only the behavior of their children that reinforces the parent's personal desires for the child. And even worse, other parents firmly insist that a child shape himself into the model the parent has created. No words can express the deep sadness and even bitterness that children develop when a parent fails to appreciate what the child really is.

Classic stories abound of the results of this tragic parental stubbornness. A mother gives thousands of signals that she wanted a daughter instead of a son, creating life-long confusion for that son. A father wants his son to be the athlete he never was, and the child has no choice in the matter. A parent demands more and more from a child until the only standard the child knows is perfection.

Both the misdirected athlete and the unrelenting perfectionist may go to their graves never enjoying the satisfaction of a job well done. They simply never learned how. And as these people become parents, the problem is perpetuated with their own children.

So you think that all normal people love to be on teams, but your child doesn't even seem to know what a team is? Write down the evidence and debate with God later. Your daughter is an expert reader, but doesn't display the love of books you had at her age? Don't worry about it—just record the facts. Your son is a great football player, but doesn't have the "killer instinct" you hoped he would develop? Your accounting skills taught your child to complete any math problem, but she just doesn't enjoy it like you do? You're trying to teach meekness, and your son wants to be a combination of Rambo and G.I. Joe? Your little girl disregards your seamstress abilities in favor of shopping for her own clothes?

In each of these cases, you should be patient. The best thing for everybody concerned is for you to accept what God has already done. Acknowledge His wisdom with gratitude. And set your child free to enjoy being the creature God intended him or her to be.

We do not make the assumption that all your child's behavior will be good, true, and beautiful. We know that

As you keep your Design Journal, look for characteristics that God has already designed, and not your own personal preferences.

the human race is desperately flawed and that those short-comings show up early in life. But Scripture teaches that God gives good gifts to men whether they are saints or sinners. It is the identification and description of those gifts that we are after in the Design Journal. The overwhelming number of notes will provide supporting evidence for those gifts. The remaining notes will be merely chaff among the kernels, and can be ignored.

Keeping a Design Journal is rather simple. You don't need to note that your child serves himself some food, but you do record that he always takes a lot of time to arrange the food on his plate. You don't need to say that your child is responsible for filling the water glasses each night for the dinner table. But you would want to notice if she always makes sure the glasses have no spots, are lined up on a tray with exactly three ice cubes in each glass, and contain exactly the same level of water.

Pay attention to actions in which your child chooses to engage. We all need to serve ourselves food, but not everyone is concerned about how it is arranged on the plate. We may be required to fill the water glasses, but not to be precise about it.

CHOICE OPPORTUNITIES

Whenever your child has an opportunity to make a choice, look for especially useful data. Perhaps she always heads toward the sandbox rather than the swings. He prefers blocks and building toys to tanks, trucks, and cars. She lines up her dolls to play nursery school rather than dressing or feeding them. He always like to surprise you from behind the door or the couch rather than to simply run into your arms. She would rather bang on pots and pans than listen to a recording of children's songs. He chooses to draw pictures rather than play with dinosaurs. She would rather put together model airplanes than make cakes. He would rather save money than collect baseball cards.

The fact that your toddler puts his blocks away when told isn't earthshaking, but when he begins to place them back in the box in the same order every time, you may have discovered a significant piece of evidence.

When you take notes regarding these tendencies, you can't yet determine their significance. You don't need to analyze them yet. All you need do is collect them. But if they add up with other items, you may establish a preliminary pattern and then seek other evidence to confirm or disprove its existence.

The Design Journal becomes a workbook that leads you into understanding your child's design. The greater the detail you provide, the greater the possibility of accuracy in determining your child's design.

The Design Journal is different than most of the baby books you may be familiar with. Many parents have gone through a "baby book period" during the beginning months of their child's life. They attempt to record when baby first rolls over, when the first step takes place, the emergence of the first tooth, and so on.

The baby book concept is a good one in that it celebrates the miracle of development and focuses attention on the fierce progress of a growing child. But most parents are so busy caring for the child that they let the baby book slide. It is rare to see such a volume that doesn't start with detailed notes in the first pages and gradually decline into a mass of blank pages.

When subsequent children review the family archives, they ask why the oldest child has a baby book and they don't. The answer is, of course, that Mom and Dad quickly became realists. They realized that the magic of the first step holds much appeal when it first occurs, but beyond that point there are many other developments that dwarf its importance.

In closing this section about observation, we suggest that a Design Journal is a far more useful documentation of your child's life than the traditional baby books. When your child reaches adulthood, it will be fascinating for him to see exactly what path he took to get to where he is. The Design Journal provides a solid foundation for continued work in

A Design Journal provides your child a wonderful historical account that will have meaning during all the years it is used.

the identification and stewardship of giftedness in careers, ministry, service to others, marriage, and family life. What an extraordinary historical gift that would be!

If you are interested in obtaining a convenient, ready-to-use Design Journal instead of creating your own, we recommend the companion piece to this book. It is titled Working Out Your Child's Design, *and is prepared in workbook format. The pages can easily be detached and reproduced if you have more than one child.* Working Out Your Child's Design *is available at Christian bookstores or from the publisher.*

Your Child As Storyteller

P eople have a natural inclination to share their feelings with another concerned person unless they have a good reason not to. When friends get together, they swiftly move past the small talk and begin to discuss the matters that are really on their minds. And when you encourage children to let you know what they think about certain things, they are probably going to be quick to tell you—as long as they sense that you are genuinely concerned with what they have to say.

It is usually possible to discover the design of an individual by having him talk about his interests. If you want to confirm some observations you have made regarding your son or daughter, you can do so with informal discussion about events you have witnessed. And your child will probably add to your pool of information by telling stories about certain events which you haven't even observed yet.

ENCOURAGE YOUR CHILDREN TO TELL STORIES

It is important to get your child's perspective on your observations, even if you have reached a conclusion that makes perfect sense to you. If six adults attend the same meeting, they are likely to emerge with six different stories about what actually took place during the meeting. Even with written minutes of the meeting, it is likely that each person would have a different interpretation about what they meant. The differences in opinion would be due to the variety of perspectives represented by each. One person interprets possible actions based on the effect they will have on people. Someone else is primarily concerned with profit. Another thinks about feasibility and scheduling. Others look at broad implications, practicality, or political consequences.

In the same way, children focus their conversations on whatever interests them, as long as the listener remains attentive. They will talk about that which is most meaningful to them and eagerly describe the activities, the sports, the play, the occasions, the projects, and the hobbies in which they can express themselves. Even though all children are involved in a variety of activities, each individual will repeatedly concentrate on certain things. You will eventually observe a consistency in what they like and dislike, and how they react in either case.

To encourage your child to tell his or her story and tell it in such a way as to be useful, keep the following suggestions in mind:

(1) *Remember that your role is one of a listener.* All you should do is hear the story. This is not a matter of your child performing or trying to receive approval. It is simply an occasion in which you show interest in something that has happened.

(2) *Ask questions to discover the facts of what he actually did.* A child's story telling skills are usually not well developed. Your questions will help the child fill in the

The consistencies of our lives emerge and rise to the top like cream, because we remember what interests us and quickly forget the rest.

missing parts. It is much like arranging the sequence of action in a movie so you can see the moves that have been made—frame by frame. Sometimes a child will spend a long time telling a story, and other times less. Don't try to make a short story longer when there is no need to do so.

(3) *Make sure your questions are only for clarification, because your child wants your approval.* He will be quick to change the plot of the story if he senses it will please you, or he will emphasize whatever he thinks you want to hear. You must be careful about manipulating his presentation. If you do not give any clues in this regard, he will proceed with the facts and, if given attention, stick to what he liked about doing what he did.

(4) *The way children tell their stories is another indicator about how God designed them.* Some children are gifted with an interest in precision and detail. They will naturally supply you with stories rich in particulars. Other children will provide high points and not be inclined to share much more unless you indicate interest by asking specific questions. Children who someday will be known for their excellent skills in relating to people will display fragments of those gifts as they relate their stories specifically to you. Others whose gifts involve skills in working with things instead of people may not be eager to spend time on the stories except in social situations. So you may find it takes longer to get what you need in one case while receiving a wealth of material in another.

Story telling requires no pressure, so treat it in a relaxed way. Take appropriate time to do whatever needs to be done.

LYLE'S STORY

Let's look at an example of a story-telling occasion by becoming a little more familiar with Lyle. You may remember him from Chapter 5. He's the one who played football to please his dad until he eventually discovered his true inclinations toward tennis. We will apply observation and story telling to see what we can discover of Lyle's true design.

First let's take a look at our observations:
- Lyle plays a lot of football in front of his house with neighborhood kids.
- Lyle's father is the coach. He's not outstanding as a coach, but Lyle still pays a lot of attention to him.
- The coach uses a lot of game plans scratched in the dust, more than you might expect for young kids in a neighborhood game.

From your observations, you might come up with a number of possible conclusions—most of which are very much superficial at this point. You might be led to believe:
- Lyle seems to love football since he plays so often.
- Lyle must be a great team player.
- Perhaps Lyle's dad is trying to give the young people a taste of what it is like to play football seriously.
- It seems that Lyle has the same devotion to football as his dad.

At this point, it is time to encourage Lyle to do a little story telling. Remember that some people will require more prompting than others during this process.

As you read through Lyle's conversation, look for any consistencies you can discover.

"Hey, Lyle! What do you like to do with your time after school?"

"*I like to fish. Sometimes I build a fort in the woods. And sports.*"

"What sports do you like?"

"*Well, I like fishing, like I said . . . and football . . . and tennis.*"

"I've never seen you play tennis."

"*I play at school all the time. No one here plays tennis. I saw all the U.S. Open games on TV just before school began this year.*"

"What about football?"

"*I play a lot of football.*"

"At school?"

"*No. Just at home. My father gets up the games near our house. He loves football and coaches our team.*"

"What do you like about football?"

"*I like playing with my father. He thinks I'm pretty good.*"

"Are you pretty good?"

"*My father thinks so, so I guess I am!*"

"What else do you like about football?"

"*It keeps me in shape.*"

"In shape for what?"

"*For tennis. You gotta run around a lot.*"

"What do you like about tennis?"

"*Figuring out a way to beat the other guy. You gotta keep figuring out the way he does things and make sure you're ready for what he's gonna do next. It's fun when you guess right.*"

"How about when you play football? Do you guess right then?"

"*It's hard because you can't keep track of everybody. But my father does.*"

"How does he do that?"

"*I asked him to use those diagrams you see on the TV football games and in the movies. He knows how, and it shows me what I'm supposed to do in the game.*"

"Is there anything you don't like about football?"

"*Yep! There are too many people to keep track of. But I like playing anyway, even though sometimes I get mad. Like sometimes I tackle a guy I don't like, just to get even.*"

"You said that you like to fish. What do you like about it?"

"*I like going with my Dad.*"

"What else do you like about it?"

"*Figuring out a way to get the fish by using the right lure. Somehow you've got to use the right fly at the right time. I know which ones to use, but I can't cast right.*"

If you were a teacher trying to determine the best method of teaching Lyle and all you had was this conversation, you might do quite well—even without all the extensive observations and stories a parent would have.

"So how do you get better at casting?"

"I watch how my father does it and try to copy exactly what he does. I also have some books on fly-fishing."

"Are the books helpful?"

"Yes, I look at the pictures. They have drawings which show you how to hold the rod and the line, and how to cast. That helps, but it's hard to make it all work together. That's why I watch my father. It's easier when I can see it done."

"What do you like about fly-fishing?"

"I like landing a fish even though it's hard to do. You have to know what you are doing, and if you do it right you have a fish. I like figuring out where the fish are biting and see what is hatching that they'll go for. I like getting the fly to act like the real thing and casting it to go where I think the fish are hiding."

"What don't you like about fly-fishing?"

"It takes so long to learn how to do it."

INTERPRETING A CHILD'S STORIES

A later chapter is devoted especially to developing some conclusions about your observations and the stories you have heard from your children. But it is difficult to read the above dialogue and not see some consistencies within this single story.

> Whenever a certain word or phrase is repeated, there is usually a good reason.

For example, note Lyle's frequent use of *figured out.* It is clear that figuring out things is a primary way for Lyle to learn. And since he enjoys problem solving, his teachers would do well to approach almost all of his subjects from this perspective. The kind of problem solving he does, however, is strategic and involves beating an opponent (as noted in regard to his tennis matches and the fish). Providing some degree of head-to-head competition would enhance the situation for him. But it is not as if he wants to get a better grade than his competition. His strategy for winning focuses on the person with whom he is competing—figuring out his moves, his strengths, and his weaknesses.

If you were Lyle's English teacher, you might want to use the debate format with some degree of frequency (depending on Lyle's oral skills). Opportunities to go up against a classmate with similar competitive interests on a literary question would get both students involved in the appropriate literature. Lyle doesn't show a strong interest in reading as a way to learn in this story, so we do not know if he has a natural leaning toward literature. Even if not, this approach would probably pay off anyway. Certainly it would work better than trying to get him to study literature for its own sake.

Even though Lyle doesn't seem to be a reader, notice that he uses his visual capability with some degree of aggression. He wants his father to diagram the football plays so he can focus on one person at a time. He learns by seeing his dad demonstrate casting and from the illustrations in the books. Therefore, he will probably understand geometry better than algebra.

How does that fact help his English teacher? Actually, not a lot, but at least the teacher could recommend authors whose writing styles are full of imagery. Illustrated versions of books would encourage him if available. In teaching grammar, the old-fashioned method of diagraming sentences makes sense for students like Lyle. Similarly, time lines will help him understand the historical placement of different literary periods.

These suggestions would apply to Lyle regardless of his age. The way he prefers to learn is true of him as a first grader as well as a university graduate student. Your own experience should confirm this. We all learn in particular ways and have always learned that way. The way you were taught changed from class to class, but the way you actually assimilated the material was peculiar to who you were and are.

We have not found, in our professional assessments, that people change the ways they learn as they go through life.

Lyle's stories bring up other interesting facts. Notice that the team situation was not particularly interesting to him. According to Lyle's own story, the team approach doesn't fit the way he prefers to work and play. Note also his strong interest in personal performance, especially in mastering specific techniques. As you can see, just these few items are invaluable when considering how to nurture Lyle in a way that fits who he is.

Remember not to reach any firm conclusions until you have gathered a lot of consistent information. The more important the decision to be made in a person's life, the greater degree of detailed evidence you want to gather.

Don't worry about whether or not consistency in someone's actions will be evident. It always is, if you know how to look.

Story Telling at Various Ages

Story telling can work for you in a couple of different ways. The first is when you ask about something you are observing or have seen previously. The child will give you some clues to what he liked about the activity and will better define your observations.

For instance, you see your son and daughter each creating some kind of structure with building blocks. You ask what they like about what they are doing. Your son says, "It looks like the firehouse down the street." Your daughter says, "It's something I made up myself."

Or perhaps you watch your nine year old and your sixteen year old each make a batch of cookies—an activity both of them enjoy. The younger child meticulously lays out all the utensils and lines up all the ingredients before he starts. He follows the recipe exactly, carefully measuring every item. You later ask what he enjoyed about making

Sometimes similar observations lead to quite different results after you encourage the children to do some story telling.

the cookies. He tells you that eating them was what he liked, and having the cookies turn out exactly the way he had planned. The sixteen year old, on the other hand, guesstimates his way through the whole project. He even throws in some almond extract that the recipe doesn't call for. When asked what he liked about the project, he is pleased that his creative efforts improved the taste of the cookies.

In both of these stories it is improper to deem either child's behavior as more or less desirable than the other's. A child's actions and preferences are clear clues to his or her individual operating style. The fact that *you* throw your own cookie batter together haphazardly is no reason to think the nine year old has a rigid personality.

You can also see how a question or two can greatly enrich your understanding of your child's true feelings. This is good to know during the conversations about school that usually take place when children arrive at home.

If your child brings home an A on a test paper, you might want to find out what he likes about getting such a good grade. Perhaps it's because he worked so hard. Maybe he likes to surprise Mom and Dad. Or because it was the highest grade. Or because he likes to know when he's doing good work. Or because he got to clean the boards as a reward. Or that he doesn't really *like* to do the work, but feels he has to.

A second type of story telling is necessary when you didn't witness the child's accomplishment and are unable to make your own observations. In such instances you are more dependent on listening, but you can still record the important points in the child's narration of the event. Listening is an excellent way to spend quality time with your child because you are allowing him to share activities that mean the most to him. In addition you are learning more about this wonder, this person whom God has inserted into your family.

> When your daughter does a splendid job on a research paper, a few questions might reveal that she loved working in the library and getting all the information, but the actual writing wasn't nearly as much fun.

Your questions are still important to keep the narrative going and to enrich the detail of the story. You can't assume that everything the child did was likable. So at some point in the discussion, if the child isn't too young, be sure to find out what he did and didn't like about his activity.

STORY TELLING BY YOUNG CHILDREN

Following are some examples of stories from a variety of ages. As you read them you will see how one child views the world much differently than another. First are a couple of conversations with a young child named Tommy.

Tommy and His Schoolwork

"Hi, Tommy! What have you got there?"

"Something I made in school."

"Let's hang it up and look at it. I like all the colors. You glued things on it. That makes it look interesting."

"You like it?"

"Yes, I like it very much. I like looking at the work you do. Where did these colors come from?"

"You know. That's paint."

"Yes, I can see that you used paint, but I haven't seen a lot of these colors in a paint jar."

"I mixed them."

"How did you do that?"

"I asked my teacher if I could. She gave me paper cups to use. She doesn't like mess."

"How many colors did you mix?"

"Lots. Some were no good. I washed them down the sink. I put some of the good ones in my drawing. I gave Billy some too. I like yellow, so I used a lot of it."

"What do you like about yellow?"

"You can make a lot of colors with yellow. I made green, orange, and brown."

"That must have been fun. Where did you get the things to glue on your drawing?"

Tommy's fascination with making colors indicates a stronger interest, perhaps, than the actual project. He puts together so many combinations that he shares them rather than using all of them in his work.

"I found some of them. I did two drawings. My teacher had a box full of stuff . . . papers and things . . . and I used them in the first drawing. In my other drawing I found things. See? Sticks . . . leaves . . . candy paper. I painted them."

"Those things look fine in your drawing. Yes, you did a fine job. I like all the colors."

Tommy and His Vacation

"Tell me, Tommy, what was your favorite thing on vacation?"

"I liked the beach."

"Yes. That is certainly a fun place. What did you like?"

"I liked the sand and . . . I like waves . . . and I liked the fort."

"I liked the waves too. But I didn't see a fort."

"I made one."

"You did! Where did you make it?"

"On the beach. I found things. I dug a hole with a stick and made it."

"What did it look like?"

"It had a roof and a flagpole. I put shells and stones in the wall. I pushed them into the sand."

"Where did you get the flagpole?"

"I found a long stick and made a flag by pushing a piece of paper on it. I made a road from the fort to the water. The waves kept messing it up. It was fun."

Conclusions about Tommy

Even though Tommy displays rather sophisticated visual organization for his age, we should acknowledge his ability without planning his future.

We are not going to conclude from these two dialogues that Tommy is sure to become an artist or architect. At this point he is merely exercising some basic motor and expressive skills.

But we should certainly take note of his interest in experimenting on his own. He doesn't seem to need more than a rough idea of how to do something. He will then experiment somewhat independently, using available materials to which he is attracted. In these two stories the objects he uses are natural—leaves, sticks, shells, stones. This may be coincidental, but we should look to see if he is drawn to similar objects in future stories.

Here are some additional tentative conclusions that can't be determined for sure (yet). But if additional stories provide further confirmation, we can be fairly sure of the validity of this evidence.

(1) Tommy seems to work quite independently of others in work and play. He needs an environment where he can operate in solo roles with some degree of frequency. Yet he may also need occasional encouragement to get involved with some kind of study/athletic/project team. Family get-togethers are another place where he can be urged to participate in a group. But he should be praised regularly for his ability to do things on his own.

(2) So far, Tommy apparently likes closure and probably would not thrive on being taken from one project and placed on another before the first was finished. If this holds up in future observations or stories, he should be given chores which don't require a long time to finish. Smaller projects, assigned one at a time, will be more geared to his design.

Tommy seems to like projects which have a beginning and an end.

(3) Speaking of chores, don't be surprised if Tommy modifies them somewhat so he can experiment a bit. As long as he gets the main task accomplished, he might do well to complete some of the smaller jobs in his own way. But if he modifies the task so completely that he really is not doing what he should, he needs to be gently challenged to focus his attention on the important things, while recognizing his natural inclinations.

(4) Tommy will be greatly affirmed if you ask for his opinion occasionally. You might check with him to see where he would put some plants in the garden or how he would arrange the tools hanging in the garage. And as he

builds confidence in himself, you will recognize that he has a contribution to make and particular abilities to be noted.

(5) When Tommy is learning something, leave room for him to make mistakes. Since he's an experimenter, he's going to try some things that won't work out. Generally, he should be given praise for getting the right results without worrying that he may have done some extra tinkering to get there.

(6) Tommy doesn't need a lot of plastic toys to entertain himself. For him, the best toys are things that can be used to make other things. And if the evidence continues to support this supposition, he should be given a workplace somewhere in the house. He should be encouraged to accumulate whatever materials and tools that make sense to him. In fact, the pattern of tools he gathers through the years may be the best display of his interests.

(7) One of the best things Tommy's parents can do is to provide lots of opportunities for him to see and experience various situations and environments. After they provide him with several options, they can see in which direction he is drawn. Then they can act on their observations.

STORY TELLING BY ELEMENTARY SCHOOL CHILDREN
Many of these things that are true of Tommy would be very frustrating to Kathleen, an elementary school student.

Kathleen's School Assignment
"Kathleen, I heard you got an excellent grade for a history project. Congratulations on a good job. What kind of project was it?"

"I wrote a ten-page paper about the thirteen Colonies. I also made a map as big as a poster for when I read the paper."

"That is a pretty big project. Did you like doing it?"

"I loved writing the paper best and I also liked doing the map."

Look for ways that Kathleen's design differs from Tommy's

"Tell me about writing the paper."

"I had to do it for my social studies class. My teacher gave us a list of subjects we could write about. We had to do one of them."

"And you picked the Colonies."

"It was the first one on the list, so I wrote about that."

"What did you do first?"

"I asked my teacher how long it should be. She told me about ten pages. She also gave me a book on the Colonies to get me started."

"Then what?"

"The next day she taught us how to do a research paper and wrote the steps on the board. I copied it down and then figured how long I should spend on each step. I had two weeks to finish it. I made out a schedule and each day I would do the work for that day. I wanted to get it done a day early in case anything happened."

"What kinds of things did you have to do?"

"I had to read a bunch of books, take notes, and line up the notes in order. Then I had to write a one-page outline. Then I had to write the paper."

"What parts did you like to do?"

"I liked all of it, but the reading was hard. I like reading but I didn't have time to read it all. I had to skip over things. I didn't want to, because the books were interesting."

"Did you know what books to read?"

"I went to the librarian at my school. My teacher said she gave her a list of the subjects we could write on. She showed me how to find the books, but I couldn't take them all home in case anyone else was going to write on the same subject. I could take two at a time. Writing the notes was hard— real hard because I was writing too much. I was going to have more notes than I could use in the paper! But my father showed me how to pick the important parts."

"Then what?"

"Then I made piles of notes according to the topic—farming . . . shipping . . . like that. Then I put them in order."

"How did you know what order to put them in?"

"I looked at the table of contents in one of the books and used that order—though I didn't have as many topics. That made it easy to write the paper. I just took the first pile of notes and wrote a couple of paragraphs and kept on going through all the piles. I ended with twelve pages and my father helped me cut it down to ten."

"What about the map?"

"We had to read our papers in front of the class and I thought it would be easier for the class if I had a map to point to when I read. In the school I used to go to, my teacher had a big map of the thirteen Colonies which she could pull down when she was teaching. I made my own, but I couldn't pull it down—it was like a poster. My mother helped me with that part. She likes art things. She showed me how to use a grid to enlarge the map out of the book. You make small squares on the small map and then you make the same number of squares on the poster board only they are much bigger. Then you draw in the large square what's in the small square and then you connect it all and then you've got a big map. It was hard but kinda fun."

"Well, we know what you liked in this project. Was there anything you didn't like?"

"Yes. I didn't like reading in front of the class. It turned out OK, but I don't like doing that."

This is only one of Kathleen's stories. You would normally want to accumulate a number of them in order to come to the conclusions we present here, but this story is a good example of how she operates. Instead of presenting a number of conclusions as we did with Tommy, here we will focus on one very important item.

Conclusions about Kathleen

It should be apparent that Kathleen likes to avoid confusion. The very first thing she did in regard to this assignment was to select the first topic on the list. Then she proceeded to ask the teacher for some direction. If no one provides the desired specifications, she starts asking questions and probing until she is provided with what she needs. Once the requirements are in place, she loves delivering what is expected.

In contrast to Tommy who moves ahead independently, Kathleen wants to know the specifications of the assignment. When she gets them, she enjoys doing exactly what is asked for.

If Kathleen's operating style isn't identified, she may undergo some very confusing times. She will be an outstanding performer for teachers who have a structured syllabus, exact goals, and clear expectations in their assignments. But teachers who have an open-ended approach to a subject, ask for opinions, and expect independent choices in projects will wonder why she "doesn't show initiative." Kathleen's parents need to be aware of this situation so that a very bright girl doesn't come to the conclusion that she really isn't too smart.

Kathleen doesn't need to be told how to make every move, but she does need to know two things: what is expected of her, and how to use the tools to get there. Once the goals are set, she is quite able to do whatever is necessary to achieve them. And if this one chunk of understanding was all Kathleen's parents got out of going through this whole exercise, they would have enough information to help her avoid self-doubt, confusion, and hurt. They could show her that not all intelligent children operate in the same way.

The knowledge of Kathleen's operating style will allow her parents to wisely insert themselves into certain situations as she is growing up, so that someday she will be a self-confident, assured adult.

STORY TELLING BY OLDER CHILDREN

Older children can reflect on activities of early childhood as well as recent events in significant detail. They can provide extensive histories rich with activities, play, people, happenings, and other things they liked. The listener is placed in a position of observing the meaningful part of the storyteller's daily living. Such memories stay vivid in the storytellers' minds because they are expressive of whom God made them to be. Take, for example, the 45-year-old man who could recall the time he learned to unlock the gate of his playpen as a child. Amazing! Even a person who treats last month as ancient history can still find a bounty of truly meaningful memories stored in his or her cranium.

Mark and His Summer Job

Let's now listen to Mark, a high schooler, recall a project he really liked.

> Don't forget: the listener always lets the storyteller direct the story.

"About a year ago I decided that I needed to earn more money during the summer than I could from just mowing lawns, like I had been doing since Middle School. I spent some time thinking about what I could do just for the summer. Then I thought about growing things, so I went to see a truck farmer about a mile down the road who set up a large roadside stand every year. I asked him if there was anything he wasn't planning to grow that I could supply him with, or anything he wasn't able to grow enough of. He was interested in having me supply several vegetables if I was interested. But he needed lots of each item, and though I lived on a farm I hadn't ever been responsible for a whole crop. So I went to my father and asked if it was possible for me plow anything he wasn't using. My father said it was OK with him, but that I would need help and he couldn't afford the time."

"So, what did you do?"

"I asked a friend of mine if he was interested in helping me. We made a deal where if the project was a success, he would share in the profits, and if for some reason it failed I wouldn't have to pay him. He had helped me build up the lawn-mowing business, so I think he thought we would be a success for sure. He had to get up early in the morning to work with me, which he hated. But he worked hard. I knew he would."

"Did you know what to do in raising the crops?"

"Not really. Our farm was mostly dairy. Oh, I had helped my mom with her garden every summer—plowing and weeding mostly—but that was nothing compared to what I had to do now. So I asked the guy I was going to sell the crops to if he could give me some pointers after I got the land plowed. He gave me lots of good advice about how early to plant and repeat crops and stuff like that. Then I got some more pointers from the county agent, especially about how to keep the insect population down. He also told me what fertilizers to use and how to stagger the planting so everything didn't come in at once. He was real smart about that stuff. So all that summer me and my friend worked like slaves—him more than me because I packed the truck and took the stuff to the farmer's stand each day and kept track of how much we were making. But my friend and I both made a lot of money that summer. The farmer's stand was on a busy highway and near a lot of vacation homes, so he had lots of business and bought almost everything we delivered."

Mark's story was presented pretty much as he told it, but we could have gotten a better understanding of him by asking a few questions. We can tell that Mark tends to engage individuals as a resource, and if this habit is repeated in his other stories, then we are on to something. Yet we also need to get an understanding about his approach to other people. The question, "What did you say to him?" would have been useful. What kind of conversations did he have with the truck farmer, his father, his friend, and the county agent?

Mark says, "All that summer me and my friend worked like slaves." What exactly did Mark do? What tasks did his friend do? What does it mean to him to "work like a slave"? When he says he packed the truck, we might assume we know what that means because we have packed trucks ourselves. But perhaps Mark packs a truck

Any older child has achieved some degree of independence and has been given the freedom to make moves outside the constraints of home and school. But Mark stands out from many others because he wants to capitalize on his opportunities.

When a child's story isn't specific enough, query for more detail.

in a truly unique way. Think about your own experience: one person will carefully plan how to fit things on a truck, another will figure it out while doing it, and still another will pile things in it without any thought. So having Mark tell you about packing the truck may prove useful—not by itself, but in connection with later information about how he organizes his room, packs his luggage for a trip, handles his homework assignments, and structures his research for term papers.

We could also ask about all the tasks he mentions. If we discover that he was involved in the weeding, we would ask him to tell us those details.

"Weeding? Why, I did that the same every day. I would get there about seven in the morning while it was still cool. I would use only two tools: a hand rake which I hung off my belt for whenever I needed to use it on some big clump of weeds growing right in the bed, and the hoe. I divided the rows up so that between me and my friend, we would have the whole field completely hoed in five days. When you do it that way and stay on top of it, all you have to do is chop young weeds into the ground. I like staying on top of it all. It's great to see it all neat and orderly, with all the rows straight and not a weed to be seen. All that summer, every time I drove past the field I loved looking at it. Funny, you'd think I'd be tired of seeing it with all the sweat I poured into it, but I wasn't."

From Mark's description of weeding the field, you could probably predict the answers to how he would pack the truck or do his homework. You can't know for sure without more evidence, but you wouldn't be surprised to discover you were right.

EVALUATING DISLIKE

Whenever you question a storyteller about what he has told you, it is usually helpful to have him identify anything he disliked about the activity. Often certain requirements of an activity need to be satisfied, but are not enjoyed by the storyteller. We shouldn't assume that he liked everything he did until after we've asked, "Was there anything you *didn't* like about this activity?"

Just as there is consistency in what we like to do, there is also consistency in what we don't like to do. When strong themes of both extremes are evident, they usually function as contrasts to provide a picture of the individual's operating style that is vivid with color. What we don't want to do is perceive these dislikes as weaknesses.

A common practice in corporate settings is to evaluate managers and then try to develop them by improving on their weaknesses rather than investing in their strengths. Yet no amount of training will transform a person with marginal analytical abilities into a brilliant analyst. Neither of the authors of this book can sing like Luciano Pavarotti, but we search in vain for a reason why that should be considered a weakness. Nor do we believe we could ever be trained to accomplish his level of talent. And just as we will never be known for our singing, other people are never going to be creative geniuses, analytical experts, corporate managers, or entrepreneurial wizards. But the lack of a specific gift should not be labeled a "weakness."

So would it be wrong to provide training that will improve performance in an area which is not a strength? Of course not. Sharpening some basic skills can make sense as long as we don't push too hard on someone without the right gifts. If a child is not a gifted writer, he still needs to develop a certain level of writing skills as a basic tool in life. We would do well, however, not to spend time and resources attempting to match his writing skills to those things for which he is really gifted. Equal performance in all areas of study and activity is not a logical standard of an educational program.

As we consider the dislikes of children, we should remember that some are merely cultural, others are a matter

Almost anyone can learn to speak French, to type, and to plan a budget. The acquisition of such skills, however, is a far cry from giftedness.

DISCOVERING YOUR CHILD'S DESIGN

As you take in all this information, the goal is to raise a child without the expectation of turning him into a man for all seasons.

of personal taste, and still others are seriously a matter of contrast—the opposites of what they are gifted to do. We know that to train a child in an area of strength will have a rich payoff, equipping the child to do that which he or she is gifted to do. On the other hand, some tasks do not align at all with the child's design.

We can discard the model of an excellent child being one who does all things well, or who is at least working on it. Rather, your child will achieve excellence as he or she discovers (with your help) the individual design that God has bestowed, and eventually learns how that design can produce results that no one else can duplicate.

CAREFUL TO LISTEN

Some people, because of the way they are designed, prefer to know the exact steps involved in their role of listener. So before we move on to ways to perceive consistencies in a child's stories, let us outline the specifics of *how* we should be listening and *what* we should be listening for.

(1) As a listener, the emphasis is on encouraging your children to tell their stories their own way.

(2) This role requires you to be a servant to your children. You must adapt your behavior to their needs rather then having them conform to a structure you set for them in advance.

(3) Let the story flow. Don't discuss your observations or try to come to any conclusions during the story telling.

(4) In order to increase the usefulness of the story, some questions probably need to be asked after your child

> A "story" is the child's account of an activity, project, or other event which he or she liked doing.

finishes. The purpose of your questions is to help you understand the child's true feelings—never to get the response you might prefer. You want to discover what your child did and what he or she liked about it.

(5) When a story is completed, ask if there was anything about the activity that the child didn't like.

(6) Don't be too quick to evaluate. Gather information from enough stories to compile evidence for your conclusions. Something that appears seven times in ten stories is strong evidence.

Now here are some do's and don'ts pertaining to asking questions after your child has completed his or her story.

(1) Don't ask any more questions than you need to clarify the child's statements.

(2) Questions should not divert the natural flow of the story. Unless they fit into the conversation, wait until the child finishes to ask them.

(3) Questions should follow the natural flow of the story. Remember that they are just for purposes of getting a picture of the action—to determine exactly what happened from the storyteller's point of view.

CHECKLISTS FOR BETTER COMMUNICATION

Here is a checklist to see if you have done a good job of getting adequate data from the story. As you grow more dependent on the child's story rather than your own observation, this list becomes more important.

If at the end of the story you have the answers to these questions, you have done well.

- What got your child started in the action?
- Where does the action take place?
- Does this action come to a conclusion or keep going?
- What does your child actually do, and how does he do it?
- What kind of people, if any, are in the story?
- What situations does your child encounter?

- What does your child do in these situations?
- What does your child feel at the end of his story?

Some stories have more depth than others, so don't expect the same intensity from every one. Since you are listening to your own children, the stories should come naturally due to your strong relationship and the wealth of available material. If you don't listen well to one story, you should have plenty of additional opportunities.

Here's a checklist to determine the quality of a story.

- Does the story portray an action your child took rather than an emotional state (unless, of course, the emotional state is tied to the activity itself)?
- Is the plot of the story true to what actually happened, and not adjusted to please you?
- Does the child provide you with a variety of stories—not all baseball, tennis, or whatever?

And finally, here is a checklist for yourself.

- Do your questions amplify but not change the story?
- Do your questions focus your child on the events of the story instead of on yourself?
- Do you know what part(s) of the story your child liked best?
- Are you continually sure that your own operating style does not prevent your child from telling the story his own way?

Occasionally we may all be tempted to tune out the stories that our children relate to us spontaneously. But when we do, we eliminate one of the most effective methods of determining their God-given designs. We should strive to be better listeners. And as we move forward, we will discover how to recognize and respond to the consistencies in our children's stories.

The telling of your child's story may be to please you, but the events of the story should never be altered in an attempt to make you happy.

PERCEIVING CONSISTENCIES

B y this point in the process of discovering your child's
design, you may be coming to one of two conclusions, depending on the way you are gifted. Perhaps
you are already excited with what you have discovered—
both from your observations and from your child's stories.
After glimpsing the consistencies that begin to appear in
your child's life, you may be amazed that you now see
clearly things you had not noticed in the past.

On the other hand, depending on how you are gifted,
you may be wondering how in the world you are going to
organize all your observations. You might see certain consistencies, yet still feel your grasp is only fragmentary. What
kind of conclusions, you ask, are you supposed to come up
with?

By now some readers will have collected piles of
observations and pages of notes. Others will have already

**As you read through this book,
you need to take into account
that your reactions will be based
on your own design.**

organized their observations into categories. Some will have a few carefully selected, fully detailed items. Still others will read all the instructions one more time before they take the first step. And some parents have read all of this and have already made changes in the way they operate with their children, but have not yet made one note. However, they will have done a lot of talking and listening.

Each of us responds to new information with as much diversity as we respond to the job of parenting itself. The only warning necessary is to not shortchange your child because of your own idiosyncratic behavior.

DISTINCTIVE OPERATING STYLE

Your child's design might be compared to an automobile's design, with specific shapes and curves—though that image is a little too static. People do behave in a consistent fashion. Yet when it comes to their design, they are always developing and growing, so we need to use words which convey a dynamic quality.

We like to use the word *design* because of its relationship to the idea of shape. We see individuality as a matter of a uniquely shaped personality. We also like the term *Distinctive Operating Style* to refer to a person's consistent behavior. In looking at your child's behavior, we are looking for those distinctives which are designed by God into your child's personality.

In discovering your child's design, you should look for consistent elements—not those which come and go because of a developmental phase due to his age. If an eleven year old's relationships with adults suddenly become intense, we cannot conclude that they are permanent elements of an operating style. Such changes should be expected at that age. But if those intense elements had been there during the more complaisant tenth year and earlier, we might come to a different conclusion. And we also need to remember that even though his intense behavior

distinctive *adj* : **1** : serving to distinguish; having or giving style or distinction **2** : characteristic

operating *adj* : **1** : relating to performing a function **2** : exerting power or influencing

style *n* : **1** : a characteristic manner **2** : a manner or method of performing or acting

may be temporary, the way the eleven year old goes about arguing with adults may be revealing.

We are not espousing a kind of baptized, vague horoscope for children. We want you to discover details concerning your child's design, and detail is tied to precision—not to generalization. You need to be able to see the characteristics of your child well enough to facilitate his or her growth as effectively as possible.

It is said that history repeats itself. Certain factors recur and condition the actions of humankind. Similarly, your child's history repeats itself because his character remains consistent. If your child is very young, record your observations as often as is necessary as you maintain his Design Journal. Each entry becomes another opportunity for a better understanding of your child's distinctiveness.

Whenever the authors conduct a seminar on the subject of giftedness, we are almost sure to be questioned about our confidence that consistency appears in each and every individual. We realize a strong desire for individuals to know themselves. The world is conducting a vain search for the great secret that will unlock the mysteries of the human race so people can know their destiny—once and for all.

We are not introducing some new truth by which we expect to cure all that plagues mankind. In this book, all we want to do is equip you in maturing your children according to the way God designed them. You can test what we say in your own "laboratory." Consistent behavior will either be there or it won't. We must simply attest to the fact that we have never met a human being who is not equipped by God with very specific strengths, abilities, and gifts.

What are you looking for in all of these activities of your child? What do you seek in the stories you have gathered? Look for repeated words and repeated actions. These repetitions will prevent you from interpreting data the way

> **As you analyze the data you have gathered, you should look for any consistencies in the history of your child, no matter how short that history is.**

consistent *adj* : **1** : marked by harmonious regularity or steady continuity; free from irregularity or contradiction **2** : having agreement or harmony of parts or features in regard to one another as a whole.

you might want to. They will guide you to conclusions that are valid.

QUALIFY YOUR DATA

We have directed you to spread a very big net while gathering data. We did not suggest any criterion other than describing the things your child has done or said to indicate some sense of interest in certain activities. You should have been gathering information without being tripped up in premature judgments about what did or did not fit. Now, however, when there is no urgency, you can attribute value to each item in your collection. There are three categories to use for this purpose.

(1) *Developmental Actions* (Activities which in retrospect were the exercise of a newly discovered capability)— For example, your child was probably involved with intense fussing over detail as he learned to tie his shoelaces. But his actions and emotions were not repeated enough to justify the conclusion that he has a strong interest in detail or precise manipulation.

(2) *Mixed Actions* (Activities which look as if they have something to offer, but which do not sing their message clearly)—Such moves are usually a combination of either developmental factors and design, or necessity and design. One factor dilutes the other a bit, but not to the point where both have no use. For example, your son (who seems to have avoided teams all his life) is suddenly excited about a basketball game in which he made the winning basket. Investigation reveals that his closest friend begged him to play, so he did. It also reveals that the precision of the winning shot was the real delight, and it came about through a lot of lonely, individual practice.

(3) *Clear, Clean Evidence of Design* (Activities in one setting that duplicate those in other settings)—When behavior at school reinforces what happens at home, at church, and on the playground, you come to a conclusion

Sometimes evidence of design is so overwhelming that you can only come to one conclusion.

because you must. The evidence shines. For example, suppose an engineer has a daughter. He has experimented and tinkered his way through the solution to every problem he has ever faced. But he discovers that his daughter repeatedly refers to a manual, a set of instructions, the cookbook, her textbooks, the directions, the dictionary, the encyclopedia, or some other written source to find answers to her questions. What the engineer might expect to see in his daughter's design is overcome by the consistent actions he actually discovers.

Our culture has a tendency to embark into the area of pop-psychology anytime they have to deal with human behavior. But in the process of discovering your child's design, there will be no confusing interpretation involved. We will not look for reasons behind reasons behind reasons for why anybody does anything. We don't discount the possibility of neurotic behavior, but that is not the subject of this book. Besides, we have found that such behavior does not prevent the discovery of an individual's design.

GET ANSWERS BY ASKING DISCOVERY QUESTIONS

When organizations use our consulting services, they often ask specific questions about a particular individual. *Can he manage creative people? Can he keep a lot of projects going at one time? Can he build a team of professionals?* A person making a career change does the same thing. *Can I sell high-ticket items? Would I like to be the boss? Can I spend years doing precision work? Can I go into my own business?*

We have already referred to the importance of questions as a method of understanding your child's stories. But at this point of the process, asking yourself a few questions can also help focus the data you have gathered. We have selected a number of questions which should be useful in getting a picture of your child's Distinctive Operating Style. The following pages will take you through some basic questions you need to answer about your child.

This part of the process is like making butter. You churn the data till a conclusion arrives at the top. And this churn is operated by asking questions.

Question #1—Is Your Child Pushed or Pulled into Action?

At the initial stage of any action, something gets your child going. Energy is initiated either from within or from without. Some children are "pulled" into the action by certain people or by external conditions. (When this happens, the child needs to be provided with such conditions in order to flourish.) Other children are "pushed" from within—independently stimulated by their own ideas. How would you say your child is motivated into action?

___ Pulled by people
___ Pulled by conditions
___ Pushed from within

Question #2—What Specifically Pushes or Pulls Your Child?

If your child is most often pulled by people, under which of the following conditions does he or she respond to the pull of others?

___ Where a leader (teacher, friend, parent, peer) presents an opportunity
___ Where a leader presents conditions to be met
___ Where an authority or expert invites response
___ Where an inspiring person calls for commitment
___ Where a mentor provides guidance
___ Where a team provides a place
___ Where peers provide support
___ Where others will pay attention
___ Where others will follow, or give allegiance or loyalty
___ Other?

You should have no more than two items checked under whatever category you choose.

If your child is pulled by conditions, which of the following specific conditions seem to influence him or her most strongly?

___ Where there is opportunity to do better than someone else

___ Where a difficult task or feat beckons
___ Where excellence can be demonstrated
___ Where conflict can be engaged
___ Where something can be collected
___ Where money can be made
___ Where abilities or skills can be developed
___ Where there is a possibility of winning
___ Where an adventure opens up
___ Where something new can be built or developed
___ Where changes can be made
___ Where conflicts can be resolved
___ Where a discovery can be made
___ Where order can be established
___ Where some form of expression can take place
___ Where performance is possible
___ Other?

If your child is pushed rather than pulled, what things are pushing him?
___ Creative ideas which have germinated
___ Concepts which have percolated in the mind
___ An imagination which has formed compelling ideas
___ Fantasies seeking translation into reality
___ Values or principles seeking application
___ Logical ideas pressing to be executed
___ Intuitive perceptions which can be applied
___ Convictions to be expressed
___ Other?

Feel free to reword any of these phrases if they will describe your child with greater accuracy. Then back up your phrases with the evidence taken from the Design Journal, citing your observations as well as quotes from your child's stories.

As an example, let's say we have a child named Catherine whom the parent says is "pulled" by a condition. Specifically, she usually takes action when there is an opportunity to do better than someone else. Here is some evidence to support the parent's observations.

<u>Evidence from Early Childhood Observations:</u>
She ignores her brother's blocks until he appears and starts building a tower. She then starts to build the same structure, keeping an eye on him. She continues to build at his pace until he stops, at which point she stops two blocks higher.

Catherine is asked to pick up her toys before dinner. Nothing happens until the warning also includes her brother and the challenge, "I wonder who is going to be done first?" Catherine finishes first.

Recurring playground observation: Catherine cannot resist a challenge to run faster, climb higher, or do better.

<u>Evidence from School:</u>
"So why do you like Social Studies, Catherine?"
"Because I get the highest grades in that class."

English Class—Discussion with teacher:
"I don't understand why Catherine is reading so much now, when the first half she just met the required assignments."
"Do you remember what you said to her."
"I really didn't say anything to her—just to the class as a whole."
"What specifically did you say to the class?"
"Oh, I just told them I was interested in who would be able to read the most books during this unit. I keep the names of the five highest on the board."

Question #3—How Much Time Does Your Child Use?

Be aware of your child's internal clock.

Each child has an internal clock which operates quite independently of the clock on the wall. Understanding how much time your child naturally consumes in an activity will help in dealing with situations where another pace is required. Read the following descriptions and see where your child fits.

A child who uses little time:
- likes a task contained at a sitting
- wants to complete a project within the day
- can produce quick results when needed
- flourishes under deadlines
- prefers immediate results
- can fly by the seat of the pants

A child who uses a moderate amount of time:
- wants to take the "proper" amount of time
- takes adequate time to get the job done
- is careful in performing tasks
- likes short-range goals
- knows that time is money

A child who requires lots of time:
- is very careful about his work
- cannot be hurried
- processes the details
- likes precision
- works at craftsmanship
- thoroughly covers all the points
- wants complete understanding

Question #4—To What Kind of Environment Is Your Child Drawn?

As you review the information you have about your child, try to discover a recurring interest in a particular environment. Here are some places to consider:

This category is more valid for older children than very young ones.

- ___ The outdoors
- ___ Workshop-type spaces
- ___ Wild, venturesome places; wilderness
- ___ Social places
- ___ Athletic places
- ___ Familiar places
- ___ Meeting places

___ Creative environments
___ Studios
___ Performing spaces
___ Educational places

Question #5—What Does Your Child Like to Encounter?

Your child is drawn to certain things or certain kinds of people. The older child has more opportunity to make decisions, and should display more varied interests. You can also expect different levels of intensity depending on the age of the child. For example, if the activity is problem solving, a very young child may work at nesting a set of measuring cups in the proper order. But a high school student may try to work on science problems or resolving conflict in a relationship.

Check any of the following phrases that are true of your child in general.

___ Likes to encounter problems to solve
___ Likes to discover disorder that needs organizing
___ Likes to work with rules, principles, or policies
___ Likes to meet someone with a great idea
___ Likes to engage information or statistics
___ Likes to get feedback, applause, or response
___ Likes to encounter a risky situation
___ Likes to get involved in situations that can stand improvement
___ Likes to encounter ignorance and supply information
___ Likes to encounter a need for communication
___ Likes to discover an entrepreneurial opportunity
___ Likes to encounter conflict
___ Likes to bump into a challenging situation (for his age)
___ Likes to encounter certain kinds of equipment or tools
___ Other?

Consider the age of your child as you go through this portion of evaluating your child's design.

Now mark any of the phrases that are true of your child in relationship to other people.

___ Likes to encounter response
___ Likes to encounter an opponent
___ Likes to encounter others needing leadership
___ Likes to encounter a potential audience
___ Likes to encounter like-minded individuals
___ Likes to encounter potential learners
___ Likes to encounter supporters or allies
___ Likes to encounter people with needs
___ Other?

As you go through these lists, add related comments of your own.

In most cases, how does your child come upon such encounters with other people?

___ Deliberately seeks out encounters
___ Encounters come as opportunities
___ Encounters are inevitable

Question #6—What Capabilities Does Your Child Consistently Use?

Close observation should reveal that young people repeat activities in certain specific areas. Read through the following list and see which area listed best describes your child.

___ *Visual Activity*—Do you see repeated inclination to read (instructions, for example)? Does your child need to see something in order to accomplish a task?

___ *Audio Activity*—Is there a need for hearing instructions, conducting a dialogue, interviewing others, etc.?

___ *Oral Activity*—Is your child regularly involved in some form of speech, debate, negotiation, counsel, encouragement, advice, command, persuasion, interview, teaching, convincing, inspiration, or similar activity?

___ *Mechanical Activity*—How comfortable is your child in working with building tools, athletic equipment, machines, vehicles, lab equipment, artistic tools, improvised tools, computers, electronic equipment, and related articles?

Be sure to consider your child's behavior in a number of different activities.

___ *Manual or Physical Activity*—How regularly is your child involved in constructing, servicing, cooking, cultivating, crafting, operating, designing, arranging, assembling, dancing, performing, or some other type of manual/physical skill?

___ *Intellectual/Mental Activity*—Does your child often use mental abilities to assess situations, compare, simplify, organize, analyze, unravel, schedule, collect, plan, comprehend, conceptualize, create, compute, implement, or process?

___ *Leadership Activity*—How is your child when it comes to supervising, delegating, representing, coordinating, coaching, regulating, empathizing, serving, counseling, entertaining, guiding, training, or improving other people?

MISCELLANEOUS BEHAVIOR WORTH NOTING

Select one or two of the following options that describe the most consistent outcome when your child interacts with other people.

___ He ends up as a leader or manager
___ He becomes a mentor
___ He becomes a pioneer
___ He makes things happen his way
___ He proves his expertise or skill
___ He ends up as one of the group or team

Now select one or two of the following answers to describe the most consistent behavior of your child.

___ Being responsible
___ Delivering whatever is expected
___ Getting things done
___ Being recognized
___ Satisfying specifications
___ Being in the spotlight
___ Changing people's lives
___ Being critical to success
___ Delivering excellence
___ Winning
___ Creating something new
___ Making a difference to a person
___ Causing growth
___ Opening up a new idea
___ Making something happen
___ Keeping things running
___ Making an old idea work
___ Making a new idea work
___ Successfully executing a plan
___ Being indispensable
___ Making more out of less
___ Increasing profits
___ Measuring up to standards
___ Affecting society/ class/ group/ team
___ Being important to a group
___ Defeating the enemy
___ Other?

Don't make hasty decisions based on assumptions or personal prejudices.

Again, let it be stated that your answers to all of the previous questions should be based on your repeated observations of your child and backed up by the child's own stories.

And now that you have worked your way through these questions, it's time to put together a story of your own. The next chapter will give you an example of what you need to do next.

DISCOVERING YOUR CHILD'S DESIGN

Most of the material in this chapter has been adapted from MOTIF ™, © 1988 by Ralph Mattson and released for exclusive use to the DOMA Institute, Number 807, Prospect Heights, IL 60070.

TELLING THE WHLE

All the nuggets of information you accumulate from the analysis of your child are like pieces of a puzzle and are genuine treasures in themselves. But the real treasure arrives when you put all the pieces together into a big picture, while maintaining a sense of how each part makes up the whole. You will not have a focused understanding of your child until you see that whole into which each part fits. The uniqueness of your child abides in the context of that whole.

For example, the parents of a girl named Jill went through the series of Discovery Questions in the last chapter. Based on their observations of her choices and behavior over a long period of time, here are some of the conclusions they came up with concerning their daughter:

- Jill is pulled into action.
- She responds to a difficult task or feat.

As you analyze the evidence you have gathered, keep in mind that this is a case where the whole is more valuable than the sum of the parts.

- She requires a lot of time because she likes precision.
- She is attracted to a workshop-type place.
- Jill likes to encounter problems to solve.
- Her encounters come as opportunities.
- She displays consistent use of precision crafting tools.
- Visual activity is evident from her research for design ideas.
- Manual activity is exhibited in her crafting.
- She is most consistent where she has delivered excellence.

After collecting these individual pieces of evidence, they are incorporated into the larger context of Jill's story. By using the above conclusions and by remembering the observations that support them, Jill's parents were able to describe Jill with the following statement:

Jill is drawn into action by situations where there are hard things to do or where there are challenging problems (for her age) to be solved. This is true about anything she likes to do since she first learned to walk, a skill she approached as a challenge with more intensity than her brothers.

Jill likes to take on these challenges where she has deadlines bearing down on her. If she has too much time, she tends to procrastinate. She is very careful in her work, even precise. She likes to use fine tools in crafting or shaping material, preferring design concepts which require detail of a painstaking nature.

She does lots of research in the library and is skilled in tracing down books and magazines which will inspire ideas. She takes ideas from these publications and

When writing out a story describing your child's Distinctive Operating Style, use all the evidence you have gathered and validated as relevant to your child's design.

greatly improves them until she innovates a design with a new and fresh approach.

Jill likes to work by herself. Though she is social, she avoids people when she is in her favorite kind of environment—a workshop or studio. She compares her work to that of others, even professionals, and likes to arrive at the point of knowing that her work is equal to the best that she sees elsewhere, whether it is wood-carving or fabric design.

As you can tell from Jill's story, her parents gathered a lot of evidence before attempting to draw any conclusions. One obvious case in point is their noticing that Jill is socially inclined, though someone who observes her only in a workshop setting wouldn't think so. And even in spite of these variations, Jill displays consistent behavior. She is consistently social except in workshop or studio settings, where she is consistently independent.

Jill's parents know they have to make sure her school situation is a challenging one, or she will have educational problems. They also know that Jill will compare her level of work to that of her classmates, so it is a great advantage for her to be in a classroom setting even though she likes to work by herself on her own projects. Ascertaining her level of ability is critical so that her fellow students challenge her to the right level. Once she is the top student in the class, there is no challenge. Yet being surrounded by students beyond her ability level would also be a problem. They would engage her interest, but also eliminate any possibility of her ever meeting the challenges.

Jill is interested in design, especially as seen in crafts. Even as a young child her parents determined to take her to craft galleries and shows in order to stimulate her interest. But once her interest is aroused, she runs on her own. She will rarely launch into a new project on her own, but she

A child's story is a working statement that can be edited and further developed as he or she matures. At each stage of development, the statement can be used as a guide in parenting the child effectively.

doesn't need close supervision once she gets started. (When she becomes an adult, ignorance of this fact will confuse her bosses.)

Jill's parents need to give her specific, short-term goals and not leave things open-ended. Her chores should include a couple of tasks which require her precise manual skills, if possible. As she grows older, her parents should give her increasingly difficult chores.

What a difference it makes to know the essentials of Jill's design! How rich a resource this knowledge will be in the future as her parents add more detail and realize the amazing consistency evident in her God-given gifts. They will have a long head start in career and college choices when the time comes. It certainly is not the only information they will consider, but it should be foundational.

When parents develop the Distinctive Operating Style statement, they use data gathered over a period of time. As they continue to develop the statement over the years, they end up with information with which they can be very confident. They have had time to fine-tune their understanding.

Use of a Distinctive Operating Style statement takes information that parents initially know in broad strokes and allows it, over time, to become vividly detailed.

Participating in the process of gathering information and coming to accurate conclusions makes the parents experts on their child. They are not forced to blindly depend on fragments of information from school testing, but can perceive which of those fragments are useful and which should be ignored. Jill's parents would find testing for academic standing very useful, given the way Jill is designed. Yet they might treat her brother's testing fairly lightly because of the nature of his design.

THE PROBINGS OF THE WORLD

Our educational institutions have put most of us through a lot of measuring exercises during our growing-up years. In addition to being ranked in all the history and math classes, our intellects, emotions, communications, sociablility, and neuroses have been weighed and measured. While some of this data is useful to solve particular problems, none of it provides a cohesive view of ourselves as individuals.

As parents, you will find that having a complete picture of your child gives you a way to measure the value of anything your child's school says. You do not simply trust every conclusion the professional may suggest to you. You know that educators are always dealing with fragments. You, on the other hand, are working with knowledge of a full technicolor three-dimensional picture. So evaluate such fragments to see whether they add to your understanding of the picture or are irrelevant.

We do not want to negate the value of the professional. A good one has experience, intuition, and other God-given gifts to help your child. Such an expert will be willing to hear your insights and invite you to be part of the team to enable your child to flourish. An arrogant or presumptuous parent does not make a good team member.

> We are usually evaluated in terms of how we compare to others, but with nothing to bind all the information together in a complete picture.

ONE MORE EXAMPLE

To give you a little better handle on writing a Distinctive Operating Statement for your own child, here is another example. This time we will take a look at Juan, who, of course, is very different from Jill.

Here are the observations about Juan made over a lengthy period of time:

- Juan is pushed by logical ideas pressing to be executed.
- He uses little time, and prefers immediate results.
- He is drawn to athletic and meeting places.
- Juan likes to encounter those needing leadership.
- He also likes to encounter opponents.
- Juan's encounters are deliberately sought.
- Visual activity is evident from the way he observes behavior.
- Audio activity is also evident—he listens to conversations and arguments.

- Oral activity is demonstrated because he advises and convinces others.
- His mental activity is clear in his ability to analyze and implement.
- Juan is most consistent where he ends up successfully executing a plan.

Adding together the previous information with other observations about Juan's consistent behavior, here is Juan's Distinctive Operating Style statement:

Juan is pushed into action by the possibility of applying an idea he has about how to make something work better or in a more interesting way. For example, Juan loves to play stickball, and will think about ways to improve the game. He will get his playmates on the block together to try out his idea. Though he is short and younger than most of them, they usually pay attention to what he says. He gets impatient if he has to wait to try out his idea, though he does not get impatient with those who oppose him. Rather, his opponents stimulate him into arguing for what he wants to do, and he usually wins the argument. He enjoys improving his athletic skills and likes to encourage others to do the same.

Juan loves to engage people, whether on the street, in church, or at school. He enjoys being a leader among kids his own age, who look to him to come up with fresh ideas about what to do with a Saturday or a holiday. He enjoys games that require a good plan in order to win. In discussion or debate, which is likely to take place when he is involved, he tends to listen more than talk at the beginning. Once he knows where the

others stand, he gets deeply involved in con-
vincing them of his position. He likes to ana-
lyze a problem or an idea and come up with
a plan that works. He also has a strong sense
of accomplishment.

As with Jill, this information is useful in understanding why Juan operates the way he does. It explains why he dislikes custodial tasks at home and why he is always figuring a new way to do something. It suggests that his teachers should de-emphasize independent projects for him and increase classroom participation, debates, and panel discussions. What Juan hears sticks better than what he reads.

As Juan matures and his parents add to the above statement, they will have a clear vision of how to help him move in the right direction. They will know how to deal with those things that block his gifts. And they can operate without expecting Juan to become somebody that he was never designed to be.

We have provided Jill's and Juan's statements for those who need examples. Feel free to state the facts in your own words as long as you include statements for which you have consistent evidence. Also realize that you have plenty of time to improve on your child's Distinctive Operating Statement. The more you observe, reflect, and record, the more sense your child will make to you. And the better you will be able to make wise moves as parents.

Based on Juan's Distinctive Operating Style, he will probably be campaigning for class president when those opportunities open up in the higher grades.

The Stuff of Everyday Living

I n Chapter 5 we discussed four categories of behavior which were assigned to help understand why people do the things they do. Almost any action can be attributed to one or a combination of these:

(1) Utilitarian Behavior—Doing what you have to do
(2) Developmental Behavior—Doing something to improve yourself
(3) Relational Behavior—Doing something for someone else
(4) Expressive Behavior—Doing what you want to do

Now that you've learned to observe and record your child's actions, to support your observations by listening to your child's stories, and to draw appropriate conclusions about your child's design, we want to return to the reasons behind your child's actions. The next three chapters will deal with utilitarian behavior, and following chapters will cover the other three categories.

Many necessary activities adults take for granted are still major challenges for children. We all go through our day-to-day routines at home, school, or work. As we do, we like to do certain tasks and are indifferent to others. But we have learned that some things simply need to be done regardless of whether or not we enjoy them.

Very young children have little history on which to draw, so they need to develop a sense of consistency and security from the repeated patterns of everyday routine.

Young children, however, go through the routines of their day with a different attitude. They need to play and to eat. But more than that, they need to gain the sense of security that comes through their daily routine of playtimes and mealtimes. Adults have developed a sense of continuity and have no fears about their daily schedules. They can anticipate what is going to happen based on their sense of history. Young children aren't yet able to do so.

In addition to lacking the assurance of daily *routine*, very young children also lack developed *motor skills* necessary to accomplish things which to adults are simple tasks. So now we have two factors to remember about utilitarian tasks for small children. Both factors will dominate their behavior, as you will quickly learn from observation.

We tie our shoes without thinking about it. But for the little person doing it the first time, it is a complicated task.

And as the child grows older, a third factor will start to show up. A distinctive operating style will start to manifest itself as the child begins to not only accomplish tasks, but to accomplish them *in a particular way.* As the child grows, he or she will welcome some tasks and avoid others, if possible. This will continue to increase during the child's growth until a full operating style will be clearly in evidence.

The neat person is a blessing in the housekeeping situation and whenever order needs to be imposed on confusion. That same inclination can get in the way when something needs to be done quickly.

If dishwashing is the required (utilitarian) activity, one child will stack all the dishes of the same size together, collect all the forks, spoons, and knives into separate piles, and wash each group before going to the next. In contrast, another child will fill the sink and submerge everything into the soapy suds before washing a thing. Knowing this, it isn't hard to guess which child can't stand having the black checkers mixed with the red checkers in the storage box, or goes into a tirade every time he discovers streaks of jam in the peanut butter jar. Nor is it difficult to guess whose closet is in perpetual chaos.

The parent supervising the dishwashing also has a distinctive operating style. The natural tendency is to approve of one or the other dishwashing methods accordingly. But the motto of the wise parent will be, "When it comes to dishwashing, who cares how it's done as long as it's done." A parent who is a hands-on manager or likes to do everything in an exact sequence of steps may have difficulty accepting this idea. But its acceptance will save a lot of misunderstanding.

In the tribal life of the home, the best results come if individual styles are ignored when not relevant and worked through when they are.

Such a "manager" parent may have been given, as a gift of God's grace, a son who is highly innovative or even creative. The parent, in an attempt to teach the boy responsibility, may assign him the chore of taking out the garbage each night. The son, because of his design, will probably carry the garbage one night, use a wheelbarrow another night, and ride it to the curb on his skateboard the next night. The down-to-business parent may not appreciate such diversity, especially all the "wasted" energy. But what difference does it make as long as the job is consistently being done? The child's variety in technique should not prevent the parent from expressing appreciation for faithful performance.

A CLASH OF WILLS

Each person has different standards when it comes to neatness—whether at home, at the office, or in the shop. We all know families surrounded by permanent mess and other families where everything has its place. Each family should have the liberty to decide what degree of order makes sense for their situation. The decision usually comes from the operating style of the leading decider, and may or may not clash with the operating styles of others in the family.

The idea that cleanliness is next to godliness comes from middle-class culture—not the Bible. But if conflict over neatness reduces the level of harmony in the family, it *does* become a matter of biblical concern.

An essential responsibility of leadership is to put aside one's personal operating style for the sake of the people being managed. This is true whether you are leading employees or children. When you find yourself in a position of leadership, you should objectively evaluate whether the necessary tasks have to be done in a certain way. And you need to know why or why not.

Sometimes a job has to be done a specific way, and the child needs to be so advised. All children need to encounter the realities of authority and obedience. They need to learn that aside from what they or even their parents *want* to do, certain tasks must be completed in a particular sequence. They must support and adjust to certain givens in life. When children fail to carry out their responsibilities, they need to share in the consequences of that failure. That is why it is important not to give children more responsibility than they are able to handle.

Other times a parent wants to teach the child to recognize and respond to authority. So from time to time the child may be given something to do exactly as the parent directs. Again, it is a matter of a child learning how to respond to forces other than his own will. This procedure works best when the child also has plenty of opportunity to do other things *his* way with some degree of frequency.

When the child is given something to do his way, try to select the kinds of tasks which call on his strengths or those tasks he chooses from a number of options.

If we fail to give a child opportunities to express his natural operating style with some degree of frequency, he will not be able to develop a healthy level of self-confidence. No one can develop self-confidence based on accomplishments in which there is no genuine interest. And without self-confidence, almost any request to do something helpful becomes an empty task.

Often such situations become an occasion for an outburst: "Why should I sweep the porch? Why do you always pick on me? Why don't you ask Tommy. You never ask him to do stuff. It's not fair." After such an outburst, the parent naturally concludes that the child is rebellious and acts accordingly—which he or she ought to, if the child is showing genuine rebellion.

But suppose the request to sweep was not received by the logical part of the child's brain. Suppose instead that it was delivered to the chamber where feelings are stored—to a place short on confidence and long on inferiority. In that case, the child's protest is not so much a matter of hating authority as it is of being incapable of responding the right way.

Who can blame a parent for insisting on obedience? Who can blame the child for feeling inferior? Who can expect such a situation to lead to anything other than greater confusion on both sides?

These situations can be avoided by providing children lots of opportunity to do good work and build confidence. All children should be assigned a number of projects that call for the strengths God has given them. And when they complete those projects in their own ways, they should receive direct communication of the parent's appreciation.

We need to be proactive about our children, eagerly nurturing a healthy sense of worth.

SHOWING RESPONSE AND APPRECIATION

Considering the amount of love that individuals need to feel affirmed, it is amazing to see how stingy people are with their compliments. Naturally, children usually need more nurturing than adults. And of all people, parents should be supportive and generous with good words whenever they see an opportunity. It is a major way to develop self-confidence in a child.

Compliments are more effective when they are specific and focus on the child's work. If you compliment a child for being "a perfect silver polisher," you can only get by with saying it a couple of times before it sounds forced. But every time you use the silverware, you can talk about how much you enjoy seeing it shine. As long as you're within earshot of the polisher, the compliment will be received each time.

At this point it might be helpful to point out three kinds of compliments:

(1) *Compliments to express appreciation for following the steps, directions, or requirements exactly.* "I appreciate how well you completed each step of this job. You must have been very patient. Thanks so much for a fine job."

(2) *Compliments to express appreciation for skills your child applied to the task.* "Look at this garage! You created order out of a total mess. I might have straightened it up, but it wouldn't be so well organized. The logic to where everything is stored is going to be helpful to all of us. I'm proud of a child who can produce such excellence."

(3) *Compliments to express appreciation for the willingness to do what you wanted done.* "I sure appreciate your doing this job. It's boring to do something that you don't like, but you did it well. You had a fine attitude and did a good job, so you are getting double thanks."

Of the four groupings of behavior, the utilitarian category has the least personal payoff because the activities are things we *have* to do. However, it is here where the parents must convey the importance of living responsibly to everyone in the family. We will all continue to face utilitarian tasks throughout our lives. The sooner we understand how best to deal with them, the better. It takes an investment of time and energy to get children to think in these terms, but it is worth the investment.

> This third kind of compliment is especially essential if the task was something the child had no interest in doing.

SHOUTING STONES

When considering the pros and cons of utilitarian behavior (doing the things you *have* to do), a Christian family might want to look at the situation from another perspective. If we take the biblical viewpoint that work—even work that we don't exactly love to do—is instituted by God, we can see that it is more important than we realize. After all, don't we believe that God is everywhere and that everything is in Him, including our work?

Since the biblical teaching is that God is everywhere, we should sense His presence in all things. Whatever we do as believers, we should do differently than those who do not believe in God. And we need to remember that nothing can continue to exist unless God allows it to.

Even when we sit down for tea and muffins, we should be aware that the cups were manufactured with

Where can I go from Your Spirit? Where can I flee from Your presence? If I go up to the heavens, You are there; if I make my bed in the depths, You are there (Psalm 139:7, 8).

Whether you eat or drink or whatever you do, do it all for the glory of God (I Corinthians 10:31).

energy and abilities provided by God, that the tea came from leaves God created, that the water comes from rain He provides, and that the molecules all mix together the way He intended. The ability to make, taste, and enjoy the food comes from God. The space we do it in and the time we use are both divine gifts as well.

The more we study the discoveries of physics and discover what time, mass, and space are, the more we must appreciate the extraordinary nature of creation. As these facts enter our hearts, we begin to view everything in a different way. Ordinary objects become transformed into special things. The "chores" we do during our daily "grind" take on exciting new meanings. We cannot do even the simplest tasks without standing at the brink of glory.

Identify the "shouting stones" in your home.

No wonder Jesus could expect the stones to cry out praises if humanity didn't do so (Luke 19:40). Those stones have their existence in God, as do the dishes we wash, the leaves we rake, the tires we rotate, the toys we play with, the tools we use, the teeth we brush, and the windows we clean. We need to come to see the everyday objects of our lives as "shouting stones"—things that are ready and available to, in some way, offer praise to God.

When we live with this knowledge in our hearts and minds, we as parents can translate it into a proper attitude toward our utilitarian tasks. Only then will we be qualified to influence the attitudes of our children as they undertake tasks for which they have no interest. Later, in adulthood, they will encounter jobs with tasks which they may not like to do. If we have provided the right background, they can remain disciplined and responsible as they approach their undesired task as another opportunity to offer praise to God.

When we begin to change our perspective on everyday events so that we see God's hand in them, we have the additional advantage of expanding our sphere of worship. It is no longer contained solely in the church. Church worship, where we offer praise as a body of believers, is then complemented by everything else we do. If you can initiate your children into this kind of thinking and living, you will save them from the misconception of most other people—that work itself is a curse.

Work began as a blessing. Later it was cursed. As Christians we can witness the reality that God is working out the redemption of joy in work, restoring that which was lost by Adam and Eve. This truth cannot be taught like another academic subject. It has to permeate Christian homes so strongly that our children are comfortable taking a different stance than the rest of the world.

Considering the fact that people spend most of their waking hours involved in work, the shaping of your children's attitudes will provide them a noteworthy and special heritage. If they begin now to look at all the ordinary objects in their homes as "shouting stones" which can be used to bring praise to God, they can continue to do so in all situations throughout their lifetimes. Who would ever think that something so important could start with the common utilitarian tasks of everyday life?

For the Christian, work involves more than putting bread on the table. It also includes the expression of the gifts and talents God has given the worker.

rules and rods

It would be a little optimistic to discuss a child's utilitarian behavior and not introduce the subject of discipline. When you plan to teach your children to do certain things they don't want to do, you need to be ready to deal with the possibility of disobedience or carelessness.

The purpose of this book is to encourage parents to nurture their children based on the way God designed them. We should tailor our parenting styles according to what is best for our children. But if that's the case, how are we to discipline them? Are we really saying that we should cater to our children? Are we always supposed to adjust to their needs and requirements? Should we allow them to get away with the avoidance of tasks that need to be done but do not fit the child's gifts?

It's too bad that the matter of discipline is frequently perceived as a clash between two parties—the Softies and

We have found that, in most cases, being a Softie or a Hard-liner is based on the way the individual parent is designed, plus a considerable degree of influence from how he or she was disciplined as a child.

the Hard-liners. Softies are almost always accused of spoiling children. Hard-liners are seen as legalists with no heart who should trade parenthood for a military career. People at both extremes claim to base their positions on logic.

We are not going to argue for either approach to discipline. Since God's plan for parenthood involves two people, there is a greater possibility of balance. With that in mind, we do much better if we look at the nature of what we want to accomplish with discipline. Then with our goal in mind, we can do a better job of determining when to be soft and when to be strict.

OPPOSING FORCES

Most people tend to perceive discipline as a means to encourage good behavior and discourage bad. But that viewpoint is not always valid. Very young children, for example, cannot yet conceptualize such abstractions as bad and good. Rather, they are experiencing the clash of their individual needs and desires with those of the community in which they live—their family, in this case.

The only "community" that a very small child is aware of is that of his family.

Young children need to learn that the community has the power to enforce its desires and to declare what is good or bad. As they grow older, they will try to negotiate in certain situations, based on their self-interests. This process will continue through their lives into adulthood as they try to attain maturity and some sense of independence.

Within the religious community an additional factor is added which affects both the individual and the community. The presence of God in our lives provides us with a standard of truth and goodness. And since God manifests Himself both in the community and in the individual, we are presented with the ideal possibility of the community and the individual affirming each other as they share common revelation.

What does all this have to do with discipline? Healthy maturity in people is marked by the ability to know when to stand for one's own individuality and when to yield to the needs of the community. Discipline should be directed not only toward specific situations, but also toward the ultimate goal of bringing about such maturity.

If parents are overly concerned with their own roles in this matter, they can become preoccupied with the issue of control. Some Christians support tough techniques of discipline based almost entirely on the issue of who has control. But in our experience, the only time control in itself becomes an issue is when there has been a failure to develop discipline in a child and we have had to begin from scratch.

Normally when parents begin with a very young child, they have dependence working in their favor. An infant or young child has such a critical need for his parents that much positive training can take place in that context. But for an undisciplined older child who has formed no such relationship, control may be necessary.

It may be useful for some parents to think less of themselves as power figures seeking control and think instead of maintaining authority. The person who exercises control sets up a potential clash of wills. This can be a problem in an environment that is supposed to nurture self-confidence and eventual independence in children. But the parent who exercises authority can at the same time show that he or she is responsible to an even higher authority. Children being disciplined by such a parent realize that they are not being expected to do anything the parent isn't doing as well.

The biblical standard of discipline is based on relationship rather than rules. This is true of slaves as well as children (Ephesians 6:5-9). God's goal is for us to "serve wholeheartedly, as if you were serving the Lord, not men." When discipline is no longer interpreted as a confrontation of wills, a different attitude prevails. If a disobedient teenager is grounded for a weekend by parents who have won a

When control becomes the issue, the emphasis is placed on the parent rather than the child. But effective discipline keeps the emphasis on the child.

Fathers, do not exasperate your children; instead, bring them up in the training and instruction of the Lord (Ephesians 6:4).

skirmish through sheer clout, he will feel much different than if the parents had explained that the discipline was to help him realize his responsibility before God. The sentence imposed may be the same, but the child's feelings are likely to be quite different.

The truth of what we are saying is tested most often in situations where the child has gifts which eventually will be recognized as authoritarian. Such children may be confrontive with others in the family, including Mom and Dad. If the parent is also authoritarian, he or she may be tempted to believe that this behavior is something that should be broken in the child.

This is a dangerous idea because the parent may act without realizing that a broken child is likely broken for life. Conversely, nonauthoritative parents may grow tired of being confronted by the child, and may even abdicate parental responsibility after a while.

Let us assume that parents have observed a consistent pattern of control in the child. For example, the child loves to tell Mommy where to sit and is delighted when she does. The child tries to make the cat stay in the bathroom, tries to make everybody obey some primitive rules, keeps count of toys, commands the respect of all his stuffed animals (each of whom has to sit in a certain place), and dislikes when the order of the room is changed or when his bulletin board is rearranged.

Parents need to act out of responsibility, not out of convenience. Children, in turn, need to learn that there are right and wrong ways to use any gift. These lessons need to begin at an early age, through experience instead of words.

These are clues, not absolute evidence, and need to be treated with only that degree of importance. However, they are very useful clues. The parents would do well to rejoice with the child when the cat capitulates, give approval when the child rearranges the bulletin board, resist any temptation to improve the arrangement, work with the child in making changes in his room rather than arbitrarily executing them, be generous with praise for the faithful execution of responsibilities, and generally provide a simple, easily anticipated scheme of rewards.

When the child's design can be positively expressed in lots of small doses, he feels no need to control building up like a reservoir that will ultimately explode. Instead, he quickly discovers that there are positive and negative ways to do what he likes to do. This won't entirely eliminate confrontation, but when it occurs the stakes are not likely to be so high.

KEEPING CONTROL UNDER CONTROL

Some parents will have a natural God-given operating style of controlling. They need not apologize unless their control comes out of neurosis rather than giftedness. Other parents whose gifts do not lean in the direction of exerting power can relax in the realization that parental power need not rest in personal clout, but in that which is imputed to their office by God, nature, and the state.

There are several factors which support the parent in these matters. Nature provides inherent authority in the relationship between parent and offspring. Instincts at work in the child favor the parent. In addition, God is the best resource imaginable. If a parent needs wisdom, it is available.

If a parent's control is the only reason a child behaves properly, the child will probably act much differently when he gets on his own. Some young people become so dependent on their parents' control that they develop no individual, internal controls.

In the 1970's, many Christian college students joined the student rebellions. These students who knew the rules openly defied them. Their respect for authority had not been internalized, and when they were away from their parents they were unprepared to control themselves.

One of the truths of Scripture is that the old covenant of obedience under the law preceded a new covenant of obedience through the working of the Holy Spirit within us. This gives us a model for two phases in the development of discipline.

If any of you lacks wisdom, he should ask God, who gives generously to all without finding fault, and it will be given to him. But when he asks, he must believe and not doubt, because he who doubts is like a wave of the sea, blown and tossed by the wind. That man should not think he will receive anything from the Lord; he is a double-minded man, unstable in all he does (James 1:5-8).

I will put My laws in their minds and write them on their hearts. I will be their God, and they will be My people (Hebrews 8:10).

Phase 1—The Law

This phase begins with the expectation that a child should obey because parents require obedience. Very young children have no capacity to understand the reasons behind a parental request or demand. They can't grasp the concept of unselfishness. There is just the beginning of an awareness of what another person really is.

At this age a child could be called egocentric since he doesn't socialize much and is quick to defend what is his. Such behavior isn't bad at that age; it's just in a primitive stage. Parents have the right to expect obedience from a child, but they need to be sure that the child is capable of understanding their commands. Before they insist that he share his toys, the child has to know what sharing really means.

A child one and a half years old (characterized as a little human motor) is preoccupied with action. To him, an encounter with a peer is much less a matter of relationship than of one motor bumping into another.

Similar behavior in a preteen is intolerable. By that time, the child has a very strong awareness of others. He knows that his own welfare isn't all that matters. He has a good understanding of concepts such as selfishness and unselfishness, fairness and unfairness. By junior high, children are capable of making judgments no longer out of parental requirements, but based on the values they have been taught and the situations they have experienced.

Phase 2—Grace

Grace is better than law, but law is better than chaos.

The phase of grace is built on experience with the law. Children need to discover that disobedience results in punishment (preferably a kind of punishment that fits the crime). If they have never experienced the penalty of the law, they cannot be expected to appreciate the phase of grace where they are driven to right behavior by that which has been nurtured within them.

An integral part of growing up is the struggle to gain independence. A young child desires physical independence so he can walk on his own. Later he wants to ride his bike without Dad holding on.

As he continues to grow, independence of thought is added to independence of actions. Decision making becomes a privilege, so that thoughts and actions can be integrated if the person so desires. And maturity is finally achieved when the person *desires* to act in obedience to the law rather than being forced to do so.

Within the Christian community, the most splendid manifestation of grace takes place when the Holy Spirit begins to guide our children's behavior so it becomes a pleasure to God. When children learn to live as citizens of God's kingdom, they can act the same when they are away from family and church as they do at home.

Parents who have successfully controlled their children for many years are often reluctant to give up the role. As long as clear black and white rules for behavior exist, a parent can get precisely what he wants without spending too much time wondering if it is best for the child. Children whose operating styles draw them to rules and regulations can be victimized by such parents. They can become so willing for others to provide direction that they never learn to make decisions on their own.

Other children have very individualistic operating styles. As they grow up and move toward independence, they probably provide a real challenge to parents who have extended police/control techniques too far. The battles which are sure to ensue are almost always fought for the wrong reasons.

While the real problem is the lack of understanding for each other's distinctive operating styles, the parents assume the issues are rebellion and spiritual indifference. The children insist that it is a matter of parental distrust and narrow-mindedness.

If a child is never weaned away from parents emotionally, the dependence on parental direction can continue into adulthood and cripple a marriage or prevent the establishment of an independent home.

THE IMPORTANCE OF TRUST

The Bible places an amazing degree of importance on the subject of trust—especially as Jesus relates it to belief. Our freedom as believers in God rests in trust. The stronger our trust, the stronger our spiritual confidence.

Showing trust in a young person is usually the best way to ensure that he or she will do his very best. Trusting children to behave in a mature fashion gives them the freedom to do so. Of course, this kind of trust can only be expected where the child has the ability or potential to behave according to expectations. But the most widespread mistake adults make in relation to young people is to expect too little of them.

A practical method of developing trust is practiced by a private school with which one of the authors was involved. Beginning in the first grade, each student is given a responsibility from a list. The list is carefully structured with increasing levels of skill difficulty and corresponding rewards. A task might be as simple as making sure that the paper clip container on the teacher's desk is always full or that a wastepaper container is emptied.

As responsibilities increase in sophistication, they might include the polishing of brass door hardware (for those who have strong physical interests), making sure the kitchenette is always neat (for someone who is good with organization), or reading to kindergarten children (for performers or those strong in relating to others). As students mature, their responsibilities become more demanding.

The key to success is based on the administration's trust that the students will faithfully perform their tasks, which is never a problem. The entire school eagerly anticipates the weekly update of the ladder of responsibilities.

When those students moved from elementary school into middle school, they were a strong contrast to most of those who had transferred from a public school. The private school students could be trusted to do assignments on

---

These issues are important to teenagers, but the nurturing of trust should begin as early as possible. Trust can be developed in increments.

At first, students are rewarded with little chunks of free time and can eventually accumulate whole periods of independent time.

time and behave without close supervision. They could easily take on independent assignments allowing them to develop even greater skill levels than provided by most good private schools.

It took a significant amount of effort for this school to design such a successful program, but the time invested was paid back many times over by the efficiency gained in all the classes and student activities. Parents will also discover that it takes time to guide their children through a modification of these techniques. Of course, they would need to do so in a way that fits their family life-style, but they will surely see rewards for their efforts. Everyone in the family will benefit from this process.

LIVING WITH RESULTS OF DECISIONS

As young people receive increased freedom to make choices, they should learn to suffer or be blessed with the results of their choices. Parents should make this clear early in the child's life.

It starts when little Kristin announces that she doesn't like what Mom is serving for lunch. Wise parents won't become disturbed with that announcement, because food should never become a means for a child to control parents. It doesn't hurt children to miss a meal now and then. Kristin can be advised in a matter-of-fact tone of voice that it's too bad she doesn't care for her lunch, but perhaps she should eat it anyway because there won't be anything else to eat until dinner.

If Kristin refuses to eat and then comes breezily through the kitchen an hour later looking for a couple of cookies and a glass of milk, she should be advised that they are not available because she didn't eat lunch, but she can have some after dinner. She may not be happy, but she will realize that she had a choice in this matter. In most cases like this one, the process will probably need not be repeated again.

Kristin is not given the opportunity to get her parents upset because they simply decide not to react. She *is* given the opportunity to make a choice (along with a warning about what the results of that choice may entail in terms of hunger).

When parents talk about discipline with children, their language should not reveal an inordinate love for the subject. Our discussions should communicate that what we care for most is the character of our sons and daughters. Not our parental preferences, opinions, policies, rules, expectations, or authority. Not our feelings of success or what our neighbors, relatives, friends, or church members think. Not a dull, dusty conformity.

Our children must sense that behind each disciplinary action is our desire to help them discover the full vibrant beauty of their interior shape—otherwise known as character. We want them to see God is sculpting a unique person out of firm decisions, moral conviction, and responsible actions. That treasure is all that can be taken when we leave this world, but it is of eternal value. And it is a treasure worth pursuing—the sooner the better!

The nature of your son or daughter began to be defined thousands of years ago as God spoke those ancient, mysterious words, "Let us make man in our image, in our likeness" (Genesis 1:26). Yes, there is incomprehensible distance between your finite child and the infinite God. But you can be sure that the One who created your child left His thumbprint as a signature on His work.

From this point through Chapter 20, we will be discussing specifics of your child's developmental behavior. As people develop, most of us like a certain degree of logic in our lives. We tend to appreciate neat answers and insist on nailing down truth as much as possible. Yet one truth that often escapes us is that we all live according to certain paradoxes. For example, we read and believe that, "I have been crucified with Christ and I no longer live, but Christ lives in me" (Galatians 2:20). At face value, it seems silly to think

The evidence that your child carries God's thumbprint is seen in the paradoxes of his or her personality.

that we have been executed and yet are alive because somebody else lives in us. The statement defies logic. Yet as we embrace the paradoxical nature of the statement, it reveals profound truth.

As we begin to understand more about the design of our children, we can also expect a number of paradoxes. We can firmly believe that a child will always act with a certain amount of consistency, and we can base our own actions on that assumption. But simultaneously we can believe that the child is always changing. He follows patterns of behavior that do not change, yet he matures and grows wiser over the years. He acquires more knowledge, skill, and experience. It is as if God directs him through all the seemingly random events of his life and continually shapes him into a unique personality, becoming ever more the person God wants him to be as the years go by.

It is is our human nature to want to keep developing as we mature. Many people influencing secular thought would like us to believe that we can develop into anything we want to become. But their assumptions aren't valid. If we truly want to maximize our growth, we must select paths of development which build on the limitations of our God-given strengths.

Much of your child's development will take place in family and school environments. The more parents and teachers can understand a child's true nature, the better their chances of success as they take him through the learning process. A circular process of influence is at work here. When you teach and train in a style that fits the way your child learns, you automatically build his confidence. His confident attitude will in turn increase the amount of energy he invests in learning. His increased effort yields more success, which adds even more to his confidence. And after you've built the momentum of learning, the child can even get through required learning experiences which don't necessarily fit his specific design.

> **We can believe that God is always the same (Malachi 3:6) but that His compassions are new each day (Lamentations 3:22, 23). We should also acknowledge certain paradoxes in our children.**

> **Teachers and parents should never forget that children always respond positively to success.**

So the challenge for us as parents is to see past the paradoxes of our children. If we don't, who will? May we ever more thoroughly be aware of each child's consistencies and continue to build on them. When we do, we will watch our children grow into maturity and completeness—each bearing God's thumbprint in a special, distinct way.

LEARNING H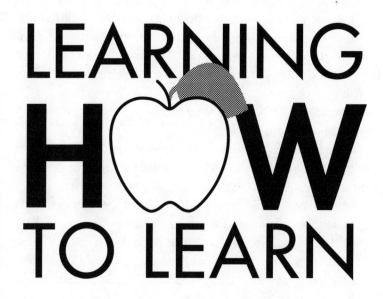W TO LEARN

Schools have the capacity to be lively, wonderful places for children to learn. But most of us have experienced them to be just the reverse. Some of the most awful experiences we can recall about childhood could only have taken place in school.

Many a mother has been teased about being overprotective and overly sensitive as she stands teary-eyed, watching her child leave for the first day of kindergarten. Some of the tears are because of separation, but many are prompted by legitimate fears. We, like her, want to be honest about any painful memories we have about being in school: doing things we hated, trying to comprehend subjects in which we had little if any interest, expected to adapt to many teaching methods which made no sense to us, having to perform in front of our peers, and being required to constantly fulfill the requirements of others (to name a few).

If you think of both the difficult learning situations and all the social struggles everyone encounters in school, it's surprising that anyone emerges with their dignity intact.

With so much at stake, it is strange that our society has devised educational systems filled with potential difficulties for our children. We are able to devise entertainment centers sure to delight all our youth, but we cannot structure schools guaranteed to provide our children with ideal learning environments.

There are four reasons why schools are not more successful than they are.

(1) *Standardization is given far more value than individualization.* Society must establish a uniform body of learning which it can expect its citizens to embrace as a matter of responsibility. Students cannot be expected to design their own curriculum (though more steps could be taken in this direction). When schools devise curricula, they do little to acknowledge the individual ways students tend to absorb the content of that curricula. This is an extremely difficult issue with no easy answers. Yet educators need to struggle with it. When our schools fail, many of our children fail. Consequently, this problem should not be interpreted as some tedious matter of educational philosophy.

(2) *Too often, teachers are not teachers.* Judging from common experience, your children are likely to encounter more people who are merely credentialed to be teachers than motivated leaders who are designed with a desire to teach. Some adults are equipped with the gifts to teach, and they stimulate genuine learning for young people. Unfortunately, there are too many of the others, who merely take students through programs.

(3) *Schools often represent interests other than those of their clients.* This is the basic problem of many institutions. They tend to be far more concerned with their own survival than the good of the people they serve. In a school, the three most important people are the student, the teacher, and the parent. Yet the status of these people is almost negligible compared to the administrator. This is a common, but peculiar, situation.

> Schools seem to do little adjusting to meet the needs of individual students. Therefore, the students (for whom those schools exist) and the parents (who pay the taxes for the schools), are expected to do all the adjusting.

> If a town has a lot of inept carpenters, nobody should be surprised that most of the houses are poorly built—even if all those carpenters are union members.

(4) *Students are seen as clay to be molded by the school.* The assumption is that schools are there to shape the student to become whatever it perceives to be the ideal student. Fine. No one doubts the influence of the school in this respect. Yet when it comes to honoring and nurturing what has already been created, there is little proof that the school is using methods compatible with the individual's nature. Schools usually demand conformity to one specific standard.

Of these four concerns, the last one causes the most problems. Even when schools attempt to recognize distinctions in individual students, it is usually in terms of IQ level or the evaluation of some other skill. That's why educators become so bewildered when they encounter students with high IQ scores and low grades. They are then forced to conclude that the reason for failure is based on psychological rather than educational reasons. But the fact is, they are not allowing for diversity in how children learn.

Some people would suggest that many of these problems could be resolved by finding a good Christian school for your child. And while we want to be supportive of the Christian school movement in this country, we have to be truthful and state that the kind of conformity which requires children to learn through overly standardized methods is just as prevalent in Christian schools as in secular ones. In some cases, this is a major feature of Christian schools.

Some Christian schools work quite hard at recognizing individuality, but they are the exceptions rather than the rule.

The thing for which all Christian schools should be commended is that students learn to associate the reality of Jesus Christ with the other truths they learn. They also discover that they can exercise the power of prayer as they deal with the needs of their school community. Both of these things are important.

But the problem remains in failing to think creatively about what it means to educate in a Christian manner and to recognize the variety of ways that individual students learn. Most learning activities in Christian schools originated

We cannot add Scripture verses to secular teaching methods and create instant Christian Education.

in secular situations. Some Christian school officials even boast that they have everything the public schools have, only better. They are ecstatic every time a Christian athletic team wins over a secular one. But these are not the standards they should be using for effectiveness.

The techniques and structures of secular schools should not be measuring sticks for the Christian school. Nor should we be in competition. Christian schools should provide an entirely different kind of community altogether, even while sharing the same objective of educating children. It's not that we *try* to be different. It's just that we *are* different.

Another alternative for the Christian parent is seen in the home school movement. Since school communities exert quite a bit of power, many parents fear that family values will be challenged and perhaps eroded.

While home schooling parents are more likely to be sensitive about the individual differences of their children, they aren't automatically good teachers. In most cases, they will teach according to the way they themselves learn or take on the role of a teacher they have known previously. But if they are willing to work with their children according to individual strengths, and if they have the necessary gifts for the job they have taken on, they can do an excellent job.

Who's to say that in certain cases someone shouldn't have one child in the public schools, one in a Christian school, and another one being taught at home?

It is not the purpose here to conduct a complete objective analysis and comparison of home schooling vs. Christian schools vs. public schools. There are too many factors to consider. If this is something you need to decide on, look at the options in each circumstance and make the decision based on what would be best for the children involved.

The more you understand what each child needs, the better you can take advantage of the options available. What is good for one may not be beneficial for another. Parents shouldn't even begin by considering the quality of the different schools available. They would do much better to first consider the distinctiveness of their children and what is required to nurture each one.

MICHAEL'S MISERY

If you could have observed Michael as a child, you would quickly conclude that he was one individual who is filled with curiosity. He poked his nose into everything—from following beetles to their lairs to dragging pots and pans out of kitchen cabinets. He took everything apart. And as he grew older, he became able to put many of those things together again. He spent long periods looking through heavily illustrated books, time after time pointing out details which surprised his parents. Mike also was fascinated with the sounds coming out of the stereo speakers and his discovery of the volume control. No switch in the house escaped his attention, and he enjoyed battery-run toys which could be turned off and on.

Kindergarten was a delight for Michael because his classroom was stocked with huge collections of toys and materials. He loved everything about school except nap time. A reading readiness program fascinated him with beginning reading skills, and he entered the first grade way ahead of his peers.

Every elementary school report portrayed Michael as a virtual genius and splendid student. Teachers loved him not only because of his interest, but also because he was a leader who had a positive influence on his classmates. Michael's parents were pleased, to say the least—especially his father who had never finished high school. They looked toward Michael's future with pride.

But something happened to Michael's performance in those middle grades before high school. His enthusiasm at school waned, even though he was still a highly energetic, enthusiastic person at home and with his friends. The rave comments no longer appeared on report cards or during

Why does a student who starts out so enthusiastically suddenly seem to lose all interest in learning?

parent-teacher conferences. In fact, his teachers seemed vaguely disappointed in him.

At this point, no one could see Michael's specific, God-given design. Michael learned best when he could physically manipulate whatever he was trying to understand. When dealing with abstract concepts, he always learned by trial and error or by sketching diagrams. In his very early years at school, he was given rich experiences to play and investigate things. At this stage, that's the way all the students learn. But for Michael, the procedure also aligned with his natural learning style. This is the way he would operate all his life.

Michael's learning style is very much like that of a mechanical engineer who experiments with gears and parts as he thinks through a way to solve a problem in the design of a machine. Michael was not unlike the British sculptor, Henry Moore, who would assemble and disassemble sticks, stones, and bones, until he understood exactly how he wanted to construct the monumental piece of bronze he would eventually produce.

There is no right or wrong about this learning style, but it *is* the way Michael learns. He didn't become this way because of his early learning experiences. He didn't become this way because his parents pushed him in that direction. He was born that way. His learning style is an intrinsic part of his nature. The influence of his early learning experiences and his parent's encouragement surely had a profound effect on him, but these factors only built on the design that was already there.

No one noticed the gradual switch from all those exciting developmental learning experiences Michael enjoyed in the elementary grades to a more abstract form of academics. When he was younger, all the words and numbers he was learning could immediately be used in practical ways. But later Michael became unable to see how what he was learning would ever be used.

A child begins to speak because he is born with a capacity to learn a language. However, the language he learns and the accent he develops is a matter of environment.

For example, how is algebra connected to most people's natural development? There are good reasons to keep it in the curriculum, but practicality is not one of them. Why would Michael ever be interested in learning it?

With the right approach, most students can be persuaded to study material which they need to learn, but in which they have no inherent interest. One approach is to reward them with something meaningful. Another is to be sure to use a teaching method that fits the way the individual likes to learn. Michael began in a situation where the two methods would occasionally be combined, and that is where he excelled.

In the middle grades, Michael still did well in the wood and metal shops where beginning skills were taught. He learned those skills not by merely reading about them in a book, but by looking at diagrams and practicing the techniques with real tools, machines, and materials. He got high grades in those courses that were geared to his learning style.

At this point, Michael's parents and teachers started to discuss evaluations and recommendations. His teachers saw low to average grades in English, math, and history, but high grades in industrial arts. They recommended that Michael consider going to the state technical school.

Michael's parents pondered the teachers' suggestions, eager not to put their son through a lot of academics with only mediocre rewards. But they also realized that after all of Michael's poking around with things, his efforts rarely led to something being repaired or built. Michael never came to a conclusion in anything he did unless it was the built-in requirement of a school project. Though they were convinced he could complete technical school projects, they wondered about a career which surely would require building or repairing.

Michael was also confused. He used to love school and knew now he hated it, even though he tried not to

Michael's parents experienced profound uneasiness as they witnessed his mediocrity in the academic situation and predicted his potential failure in a technical environment. He had started out as such a good student.

show it. He hated losing his leadership role. He hated the fog that seemed to descend on his mind as he tried to focus on the classroom lectures. He used to love books, but because of all his required reading he now hated them, too. He couldn't understand why his teachers patronized him. He dreaded getting back test papers and receiving report cards with all those evil marks on them.

Michael might have just given up, but he had a strong attraction to two of his teachers. They not only kept him going, but eventually became just about the whole focus of his time in school. Curiously, the teachers Michael admired were his art teacher and science instructor. He knew those two teachers kept a friendly battle going as each one teasingly put down the other's subject. But the two of them became allies in their enthusiasm for Michael's success. Michael produced brilliant work for both of them.

Other faculty members attributed Michael's suspiciously high grades in those classes to partiality from two overly enthusiastic teachers. While they were glad that Michael could be encouraged in art and science, they did not see his grades in those courses as significant—especially since only one of them was academic.

The school psychologist offered to give Michael an IQ test, but he refused. He couldn't stand to get another disappointing "grade," and didn't want another professional opinion about something that everybody already knew to be true: He was a neat kid but a below average student. Michael didn't want to be average, much less below average. In fact, he didn't want to be compared to anybody.

GETTING TO THE ROOT OF THE PROBLEM

Michael's parents finally became fed up with the inability of the school to bring an end to Michael's unhappiness. They suggested a private school which could give Michael more individual attention. Michael had no intention of displaying his mediocrity in front of a new group of people, and he

> Whenever Michael walked into the science or art classroom, all the pressures disappeared. He became almost light-headed as he surveyed the equipment, tools, and materials to be explored in each.

became angry at the suggestion. His parents pulled rank. They insisted that they had no intention of paying for something he didn't want to do, but also thought Michael should base his decision on evidence and not just personal feeling. They left it up to him to make a logical decision.

Michael reluctantly agreed, and he shared his concern with his science and art teachers. Both surprised him with their delighted support for the idea and offered to provide recommendations. With this response, Michael visited the private school to check it out for himself.

Michael eventually decided to apply, and his art and science teachers were quick to stop by the Admissions Office of the private school. They convinced the school officials that Michael was a potential gem if the school could tailor the right educational experience for him. They formed a rough plan that, in its essentials, recognized Michael's explorative hands-on nature.

Michael's whole attitude toward school was revolutionized. The science department took a special interest in Michael, proceeding to make him work hard and finish each reading assignment with extensive explorative lab work. Other instructors also adapted to Michael's learning style. And Michael soon discovered that he was able to do excellent work if he went at it in a particular way.

The private school tried to minimize every student's fears about being inadequate by having the philosophy that, "Each pupil is in the best seat."

Michael continued in private school for two years, until the financial burden became too great for his parents. When the news came that he had to complete his secondary education in public schools, he admitted to some fears. At the same time, he knew that he was now a capable student and expected to do nothing but good work.

The public school still did little to adapt to an individual's learning style, and it was somewhat difficult for Michael to keep up the same level of grades. But by now he knew how to make those adjustments himself, and he had the confidence to maintain good quality. It wasn't as much fun, but he was able to keep his grades up.

Eventually Michael became a physics major on scholarship at an excellent university. And he developed a love for something he was truly good at—research. As it turned out, this type of pure research was a sophisticated form of all he had done as a kid at home. He found himself wonderfully caught up in projects which hardly ever came to an end, and in which he was always learning and discovering.

CONCLUSIONS

Consider how much pain Michael and his family could have been spared if his teachers had paid closer attention to the way he is designed. It is alarming that such a community could have endangered his gifts and his joy—to say nothing about his potential fruitfulness. Fortunately, Michael was blessed with a couple of teachers who knew his problem was a matter of adjusting to a particular learning style. If they hadn't helped unravel the situation, Michael may have been placed into psychological therapy, a response that would have made the situation twice as confusing.

> The school should serve the student. The student should serve the school. But the student should never be the servant of any system.

As a parent, you first need to understand how and why your son or daughter learns. You then need to protect that learning capability from those who insist that everyone should learn in the same way. In addition, you need to gradually make your child aware of how he learns so that he can function in settings that go against his natural style.

We don't need to cater to our children in unrealistic ways. But the power of education can be increased by working through the strengths of the students we serve. Students will find plenty to adjust to in school without our adding unnecessary burdens.

NOTORIOUS WORDS

T his chapter is written as a short lexicon of comments commonly heard from educators in regard to students who don't conform to the instructor's ideal model of what a student should be. As a parent, you are likely to hear one or more of these statements as your child goes through the school system. Don't panic if you do. You know your child better than the teachers. Below each comment is a paragraph or so to help you better interpret the truth about your child in the situation. We begin with the most famous statement of them all.

"I'm afraid, Mrs. Johnson, that your son is just not motivated."

The truth is that Mrs. Johnson's son is highly motivated, but not necessarily to do what his teachers want him to do. The very same teachers who came up with this evaluation could

When you can, help a child accomplish something he doesn't want to do by capturing his enthusiasm for something he *does* like to do and folding it into the rejected activity.

surely describe a host of the boy's achievements outside the classroom that required generous amounts of energy and motivation. A genuinely unmotivated student wouldn't have the stamina to survive the disapproval he seems to receive from his instructors.

"I'm afraid, Mrs. Johnson, that your son is just not motivated to learn."

This statement is a slight variation of the previous comment, and just as erroneous. The activity of learning is the only way young people can mature. God has designed all people—*especially* young people—to be learners. Learning is the most powerful motivating force in education. The key, however, is in knowing *how* the individual learns. Mrs. Johnson's son is constantly learning all kinds of things, but he may have difficulty generating enthusiasm for subjects in which he has no interest or those unrelated to his life.

"Your daughter doesn't seem to be able to work independently without bothering others."

You should be aware of the norm that is assumed in this statement. Yes, some students are inherently put together in such a way as to enjoy doing things on their own. They will prefer skiing over basketball any day. But it is also true that others will automatically gather a team around them whenever a project comes up. Your daughter shouldn't suffer because she is in the latter category. Team players will be in demand in many situations she will encounter in the future. Don't let her establish a misconception early in life.

> Does it really make any difference whether learning takes place solo, duet, or in larger groups—as long as it effectively takes place?

"Your son doesn't seem to trust his own judgment. He constantly asks his teachers if he is doing the work right."

Sometimes a youngster lacks self-confidence, in which case some strategies need to be developed to provide assurance of his worth. But more often a comment like this one is directed toward an individual whose gifts make him inclined to deliver results according to specifications. When a teacher makes her expectations clear, there is no problem. But teachers need to realize that this kind of student will always struggle with open-ended assignments.

If a teacher expects a requirements-oriented person to respond well to open-ended assignments, she is expecting a lark to bark. That's not how God created larks.

"He is always clowning around in class. I will not tolerate it."

Many adults who are now leaders of industry, entrepreneurs, and in a number of people-oriented professions describe themselves as having been class clowns. Misbehavior during class certainly needs to be addressed. But what is so wrong about the desire to have a direct effect on others, to make them laugh, to cheer them up, or to change their behavior? People who motivate other people will someday be of great value to employers.

"She only gets things done when given step-by-step directions."

Again, who is to say that this behavior is any worse than someone else's who spends a great amount of time pursuing dead ends until finally arriving at the right solution on his own? Some people like keeping a half dozen balls in the air; others like to focus on one thing at a time, get it out of the way, and then move on to the next project. Some students like to wing it; others like to follow exact procedures. All are designed by the same Creator. How can we say that one is right and the other is wrong?

"Your daughter has to be called on in class. She never volunteers on her own."

Are we to assume that it is normal for people to volunteer to give answers in class? Some people like to play the role of an expert; others do not. Some like to make presentations to groups; others hate to speak in public. We are not suggesting that students should never deal with the skill of speaking in front of others, but we should not make her

Change is most promising in cases where the individual is set free to do whatever he or she has been equipped by God to do.

eagerness to be so involved a measure of emotional health. Nor should we assume that those who have no interest in public speaking will change their attitude through practice.

It is better to recognize such disinterest as natural to many people, with the teacher showing how to do the best job possible when it is necessary to speak before others. Genuine change is possible where trauma has gagged someone gifted to speak before groups. In such a case, practice makes a lot of sense once the gag has been successfully dealt with.

Whenever you hear negative comments about your child, you don't want to disregard them. Some of them may be true at face value, and you will need to respond. But even if your child's teachers don't have a complete understanding of his or her distinctive operating style, their comments are still valuable. While such comments may not be the entire truth, they will certainly reveal clues about the child's true design. At that point, you as a parent can take appropriate action. As you see past the misperceptions, you can minister to your child in a way perhaps nobody else can. And you will both benefit from the experience.

At no point are we suggesting that a child is someone to whom we all must adjust. But we *are* warning against the idea that we can coerce our children into becoming someone other than whom God created them to be.

YOUR CHILD'S LEARNING

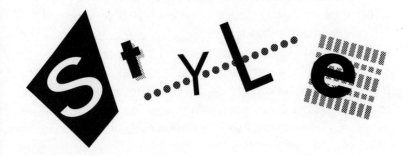

A number of professionals in the fields of people behavior and education are more than generous in their criticism of today's educational system. Some of the authors' own misgivings have no doubt leaked into the content of this book. Our desire is to stimulate educators to think in fresh ways about the nature of what they are trying to accomplish in the lives of young people. But an even more pressing goal is to help parents support and protect their children, no matter where the children are going to school.

The modern school has a very narrow focus on logical, problem-solving abilities and verbal intelligence. Students who are naturally drawn to this emphasis can do very well and will be strongly affirmed by the reward systems of the school. But students whose inherent strengths find no natural expression in the structure of the school

No wonder so many adults seem unhappy. Their jobs, which they don't enjoy, are like extensions of school, which they didn't enjoy either!

system will wonder about their value as persons. The best things they have to offer—the very gifts for which God has designed them—are no more than casually appreciated.

Many of these unappreciated students will still perform well and will provide exactly what is required of them—out of conscientiousness, obedience, or a strong family value system. But all their effort will result in little personal meaning, and almost no recognition of value. It is all, in a sense, busywork. It has little to do with the realities of life. It provides no electricity or enthusiasm, and students feel no excitement about becoming more mature.

The ability to succeed in school depends primarily on gathering, retaining, and applying information. This is done mostly through reading books, listening to teachers, and organizing the information. When your child is free to do whatever he is inclined to do, it won't take long for you to observe what information interests him and how he goes about gathering it. Obviously, children who have their noses in books and like to talk about what they read are going to do better in most school situations than those who learn by handling and experimenting with things.

EXAMPLES OF INDIVIDUAL LEARNING STYLES

In this chapter we want to examine several different ways that young people gather information and begin to apply it. After describing each category, there is a brief section on how you can best help that child learn.

"Show me how, Dad."

A child in this category doesn't learn how to ride a bicycle by trying it out on her own, but wheels it into her father's presence and asks him to demonstrate. One of the first toys that attracts attention might be one where certain shapes must be inserted into similarly shaped holes. An individual who absorbs information visually will be drawn to any toys that promote that style of learning.

When learning the computer, the manual will be worthless to this kind of child for anything other than a doorstop. She will wait for someone to show her what to do. And when she is shown what to do, she will learn quickly and perhaps outdistance anyone else in her class. But this won't guarantee a good grade, because the test will probably be based on the computer manual.

HOW TO HELP: In all subjects, encourage labs, workshops, projects, and the use of diagrams. Show her how to survive literary subjects by transforming book plots into mental movies (something she can "see"). Coach her through discussion roleplay to prepare for classroom discussions. Do not assume that her leaning toward visual learning will prevent her from understanding high levels of abstraction. But you will probably need to make sure the learning methods for such lessons are "visual" enough to be of help to her.

"My math teacher is the greatest!"

The "show me" person needs others to demonstrate how something is done, but could learn just as well from a videotape as from a live presentation. Other students need the human element of a mentoring relationship that combines content with personality. This student will have strong interpersonal skills and will care more about the approval of the mentor than the grades received. From early childhood, this type of person will involve others and tend to apply himself to whatever degree encouraged by the mentor.

For this type of student, the pattern of grades will not necessarily correspond with subject interest. Ordinarily you might expect high grades in one category of subjects and lower grades in another (for example, math and science vs. history and English). Rather, this kind of student will do well in the classes where the teacher shows concern and interest toward the student.

This student flourishes under the tutelage of teachers who take a direct interest in students who show strong interest.

HOW TO HELP: Parents need to show strong personal interest in what is happening to the child in school. This type of student tends to do better in small schools with a strong sense of community, and where teachers are able to be close to the students. In high school, care needs to be exerted in terms of college and career counseling. The student might be drawn to an area taught by a favorite teacher—whether or not the subject is one in which the child is gifted.

"I love homework!"

A love for homework suggests a love for learning—not only about favorite subjects, but about a number of things. A parent with this kind of child might not expect him to have problems with school. Usually these children do very well, but they can quickly become overwhelmed with so much information to absorb. They are tempted to do more than necessary with open-ended assignments, such as research papers. They do not find it easy just to skim through texts which deserve nothing more.

> These students cannot be diverted easily from books which fascinate them. This would be good, except that they find more of these books in a month than most people can read in a lifetime.

HOW TO HELP: This type of child is virtually incapable of assessing how much value or time should be attributed to an assignment. Parents can help by providing realistic schedules and preventing too much burning of the midnight oil when sleep would do more good than a third rewrite. In most cases, the child won't outgrow the need for guidance in regard to organizing time and energy. During the junior and senior years of high school, some thorough career and college planning needs to take place. It is very easy for this kind of person to continue his love for learning by getting one degree after the other, with no consideration of how the learning applies to career goals.

"Let me try it."

Some people prefer to learn by doing. This type of child always wants to get into the action and does well in the lower grades. Later he or she may find academic subjects rather tedious, unless they involve experiments. Such students flourish in a laboratory environment. Otherwise they feel a desperate need to fend off the conclusion that school is dumb and so are they. It helps whenever these children also show a natural inclination toward competition or being an outstanding performer. The potential for rewards may justify the pain they risk by taking on academic subjects.

HOW TO HELP: The tricky role for parents here is not to defend the school too strongly. Their child needs parents who will appreciate difficulties when they come. And while parents shouldn't measure the child's worth by grades, the child doesn't expect the parents to ignore low grades, either. Tutoring which features diagrams, experiments, demonstrations, and any other hands-on opportunities can make a big difference.

"Let me play with it."

The difference between this category and the previous one is the purpose of the child's efforts. Previously, the goal was to acquire knowledge. In this case, the child wants to tinker his way to the solution of a problem or the invention of a new idea. This kind of person is more interested in creativity or putting together interesting possibilities than he is in coming up with a solution. As very young children, people in this category were the ones who figured a way to unlock barrier gates and escape from playpens. When they got a little older, they loved getting puzzles for gifts, as well as any kind of building toys (blocks, Legos, Tinker Toys, Play-Doh, etc.). But they never built anything pictured in the instruction booklet. They always came up with their own special creation.

For a child in this category, the payoff in learning is the discovery of something new.

HOW TO HELP: In most cases, this kind of child can pretty much be turned loose to learn on his own. He doesn't need much outside stimulus. The best thing a parent can do is keep him supplied with generous supplies of stuff which can be handled, used for building, changed, or reshaped. As the child gets older, he will discover his own sources of creative materials. He will need sympathetic support when assigned to noncreative teachers. Time drags on and on in such an environment.

"I've got to do it right."

Learning is important to this kind of child, but it isn't always fun. When learning is required, this individual wants to know the details of the assignment so he can do it exactly right. Open-ended classes are dreaded by these students, as are projects with many options. This person wants to know what the teacher expects, and shows little enthusiasm for sharing his or her own opinion. Rules, regulations, structure, and grades provide all the parameters this kind of student needs.

HOW TO HELP: Well-meaning teachers may sometimes try to change this kind of person into a creative individual by providing innovative possibilities. But that may not be what the child needs. These children do not need help with their schoolwork unless it is beyond their skill level. Adults just need to keep an eye open to make sure the child isn't getting in over his head. Another requirement for children in this category is clear communication. They need to know exactly what is expected of them at home and they need to receive clear signals of appreciation when those expectations are fulfilled.

NO BOXES, PLEASE

The previous categories should not be used as a set of boxes in which to drop your child. To do so would be unfair to the facts and, more importantly, to the child. The above list is not exhaustive, and is given to provide you with a few examples.

Don't start with these categories and then try to find your child's learning style. Start by looking at how your

God blesses some people with these orderly gifts as a barrier against barbarism and chaos.

If you compare each "How to Help" section with the way that type of child learns, you will have a number of models to help you develop your own support strategy.

child actually goes about learning in all the years he or she has been in your house.

All of us learn from our day-to-day experiences, and we mature. That kind of learning is universal, even though the actual process differs from person to person. Here we have focused on the way a child learns in formal situations. In such circumstances, not everyone operates out of a desire to learn.

In addition to the previous descriptions, there are many other styles which operate in the school situation. Grades are often achieved in order to please Mom, Dad, and teacher. Some people want to be the most outstanding student. For others, school is a competitive challenge—not unlike a football game.

Whatever drives your child's scholastic life, don't lose sight of his strengths.

You should encourage each child to use his strengths, never attempting to change them. (It would be a vain attempt anyway, because it would be going against what God has supplied.) As your child matures, the real issue will shift from the nature of the gift to rest ultimately on the person's relationship with the gift giver. That relationship will be part of the focus of the next chapter.

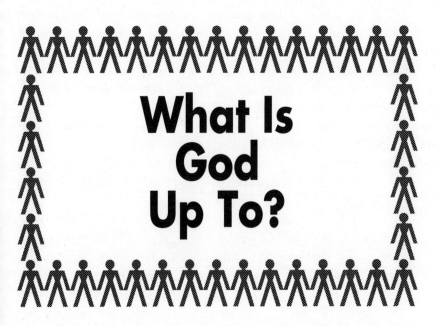

What Is God Up To?

In our discussion of how to nurture our children effectively, we need to include a chapter on relational behavior. We are individuals thrust into the interactions of society, and we soon discover how important relationships with other people are to us.

We have our origins as embryos within a person. We are first nurtured into a knowledge of ourselves by a family—more persons. We spend all our years on earth dependent upon other persons—psychologically, spiritually, socially, emotionally, politically, professionally, and practically. We also discover the great fact that we are accountable to a Person who is the source of our own personality, who is above all other persons earthly or heavenly. What is God up to?

The first persons on Earth, Adam and Eve, knew what it was like to experience sparkling clear communication.

It is obvious that how we relate to persons is a matter of colossal importance.

DISCOVERING YOUR CHILD'S DESIGN

They weren't limited by the flaws which encumber today's attempts to understand each other. They even enjoyed a one-on-one personal communication with God. But the fall of man destroyed those clear communications, both with God (vertical) and with one another (horizontal).

Today we don't always have adequate information to determine how another person thinks. Consequently, we have the tendency to assume that whatever is true about ourselves is true about everybody else. We tend to believe that everyone else needs from relationships the same things that we need. We also believe that *how* we relate to others is how everyone else should relate.

The individualistic person thinks that those who love groups and teams haven't yet learned to get along on their own, and that when they mature emotionally they won't be so dependent upon others. The team players wonder when their loner friends are going to shuck their neurotic self-centered behavior and enjoy the company of others. This ignorance on both sides seriously distorts the way we relate to each other. Add to that our self-centered ambitions, and between the two we have a huge potential for confusion every time we talk to each other.

We often miss the fact that each person has within him a design that draws him to particular kinds of relationships. In addition, there are four dynamics which influence the way we operate within the relationships to which we are drawn:

(1) *Developmental History*—What you are taught about relationships during your critical early years.

(2) *Communal Needs*—The fact that everyone must make adjustments to other people.

(3) *Influential Style*—Unique gifts which emerge because of the way God has designed each of us.

(4) *Concept of God*—A spiritual perception that affects your social relationships.

> **When it comes to relating to others, we automatically conclude that our way is the right way.**

> **These four factors will influence every relationship you (and your child) will ever have.**

A book could be written on each of these four dynamics. But at this point, we want to deal briefly with each of these factors in order to stimulate ideas and to provide a checklist to help you organize your thoughts about your own children.

DEVELOPMENTAL HISTORY

The relational growth of a child depends from the very beginning upon his link to his mother. This is indispensable. The bond of mother to child and child to mother is the foundation of all that follows in life. During the first year especially, the infant needs to experience security. This feeling of security is needed before the child can ever venture forth and begin to differentiate himself from others. Then if any of the child's encounters with people make him uneasy, he can return to the security of Mom until he's ready for a new venture.

In this way the infant moves from his total dependency on Mom and begins gradually to identify others and even imitate their facial expressions. This capacity to appreciate others increases until some genuine empathy will be evident. For example, the child will cry when another child is in misery. And by his second year, the child will respond strongly to both affirmation and disapproval.

A young child's natural inclination to imitate other people reveals that something within him is preparing him to understand the moods of others.

Between the ages two and five, the child makes more sophisticated advances. He is able to learn letters, numbers, words, and pictures. His capacity for understanding symbols allows the use of personal pronouns, which further clarifies the differences between himself and others. How the family teaches those symbols influences all subsequent uses of the words *me* and *you*. And the frequency with which each of these words is used will affect many of the child's future relationships—both with other people and with God (in whose image the child should find his identity).

Another aspect of a developing person is sexual identity, which takes place by age five. This is an especially

Most adult sexual identity problems have their roots in some kind of unrecognized disturbance during these early years.

important element of understanding oneself—so important, in fact, that any distortion is likely to be permanent outside of its eventual healing by the Holy Spirit.

The years between birth and age five are enormously important in equipping us, for the remainder of our lives, to engage in healthy relationships. The church could find fewer ministries of greater importance than to equip new parents to fulfill their roles during these critical, tender, and indelible years of their children's lives.

COMMUNAL NEEDS

God has never been nor can ever be lonely, because He eternally enjoys the society of His own Trinity. So in a sense, God is His own best company. We, being made in His image, carry in us some of that same social nature. In fact, all of us are so social that we cannot discover our selfhood outside the context of knowing others. Therefore, even the loner, by temperament, is inherently social by nature. He cannot develop in isolation, though he may choose to live in some degree of isolation after he develops. (The unanswered question is if he can continue to develop outside the community.) One of the most important contributions any of us can make toward others is to be expressive about our appreciation for who they are.

There can be no knowledge of self outside the experience of knowing others and how they value you.

In the case of our children, it is important for them to appreciate the various communities they belong to—church, town, family, and nation. Through these communities they learn what it means to be a citizen. They discover what it means to receive practical services and develop a sense of place and identity. They learn to give back unselfish sacrifice and service. They deal with the issues of individual rights versus the rights of others. They discover, in a practical way, something of what Jesus meant when He said that to save your life you must give it away.

When communal response to a child is enthusiastic and supportive, it enables children to discover selfhood and worth. The most essential of all communities is the family. This group exercises the strongest power to set the individual free to be his own person, and thereby to relate freely to others. The child, in turn, must learn the value of the communities and become a productive member himself.

INFLUENTIAL STYLE

A school-age child who has been adequately trained to socialize by his family can independently establish a number of friendships. And from that point, the way your child relates to school and to his new friends depends on his influential style.

Do you remember how your child made his entrances when he was younger? Some children thrust themselves into the company of adults like a bomb exploding. Others quietly slink into the group.

Your child's behavior in this and similar situations characterize his design. And no matter how the influential style of that design expresses itself, it is probably a permanent characteristic which years later will be a factor as the child considers career options.

People may express their influential styles in a number of ways. Mary is a leader; Bill is a highly supportive follower. James almost always treats others like an audience while his brother can work for hours by himself. Darren organizes the troops while Carol organizes herself. Tony charges everybody with enthusiasm; Kathy funnels it into action. How they interacted with people in the past is, for the most part, how they will interact with them in the future—only with increasing degrees of sophistication.

The school-age child moves into relationships with a new ingredient added to those of earlier years. Now there is a strong awareness of talent and capabilities, and an interest in displaying competence. So this is an age when identity is very much tied to performance. It is not enough for the

The time comes when identity becomes very much tied to performance. It is no longer enough to know oneself.

child to know himself. There is also a need to express himself with observable results so peers can recognize his value and provide affirmation.

Because of this need, there are two important things that parents should do. *First, you should support the natural connection between the value of the child and the quality of how he performs.* When a child performs inadequately or fails at something he attempts, well-meaning parents might be quick to say, "It doesn't make any difference. Your worth has nothing to do with your performance." But that's not what the child wants to hear. The very shape of our physical bodies indicates that we are made to work and accomplish things. The fact that we are created by God with a unique set of gifts directs us toward certain kinds of work. When our gifts are applied to the right kind of work, they produce excellence.

It is the nature of the human being to demonstrate his uniqueness by doing good work in his specific area of giftedness.

When God created the world, He commented favorably about His work. When your child (made in the image of God) accomplishes something, he needs to be able to attest frequently that it is good work. And we can avoid false pride as long as we realize that all gifts, abilities, and talents are given by God. It is important to operate as stewards of the things God has given us in our work, leisure, and service. And someday we can hear the most favorable comment of all about our work: "Well done, thou good and faithful servant."

We are God's handiwork, created in Christ Jesus to devote ourselves to the good deeds for which God has designed us (Ephesians 2:10, NEB).

Second, you can encourage your child to find activities where he can really excel. This is possible only as you become aware of his individual operating style. It is no blessing for children to be placed in situations where they cannot perform well. And since they are often overly influenced by peers, they may not always identify nonproductive situations. The parent can help prevent the child from going through a lot of misery.

In summary, your child has a consistent way of relating to others when he has a choice about the matter.

Learning to appreciate that style will help you remain supportive, always anticipating the best way to relate to him in
any given situation. Parents also need to recognize achieve-
ment so their children will be secure in relating to others,
especially their peers.

THE CHILD'S CONCEPT OF GOD

The fact that God has initiated a relationship with us casts a
different light on all other relationships. Young children
cannot understand this very well, since the entire concept
of relationships is new to them. Yet parents can nurture
children in an understanding of God's mercy, grace, and
forgiveness. This understanding gradually increases until, in
their teen years, young people are able to better appreciate
what it means to be forgiven of sin. Consequently, they are
more capable of forgiving others.

Training children is most effective when our instruction is accompanied by mercy, grace, and forgiveness. We must toss aside the idea that parents are supposed to present themselves as perfect people.

Christian parents can become self-conscious about
their responsibility to train children to have a relationship
with God. Sometimes we do a lot of talking, teaching, and
reading about God, but provide children with little *experience* with God. Sometimes parents feel as if they have a
greater interest in their children's relationships with God
than the children have—perhaps even more than God
Himself has. And since children tend to fulfill parental
expectations, they are likely to deliver the minimal level of
spiritual interest anticipated by the parents.

As might be expected, the parents sometimes feel that
they are guilty of a shortage of faith. But rather than berate
themselves, they need to keep three things in mind:

(1) *God anticipates our need.* He will definitely recognize and respond to our lack of faith. He will bolster our
confidence in Him and in His divine appreciation for each
of our children.

(2) *God will initiate spiritual growth.* As we aggres-
sively claim that we want our children to develop a strong
relationship with Him, God will readily respond with an

explosion of spiritual repercussions to help both children and parents reach that goal.

(3) *God knows more about our children than we do.* He is already active in the secret corners of their lives in ways we know little about.

As their children mature, parents shouldn't be content to indoctrinate them into an understanding *of* God; they should initiate children into experiences *with* God as well. Children should see God more clearly through the door of their own parents' relationship with Him. Children don't find it hard to believe that God is really there when they see the confident ways that parents walk and talk with Him, handle fears, respond to hard times, deal with illness, feel security within God's love, and enjoy His presence. Parents won't find it difficult to nurture a child spiritually if the child has already been shown that God is easily accessible.

> Indoctrination takes place when we confront our children. Initiation takes place when we confront God and allow the children to witness the encounter.

A TEST FOR THE READER

Read this next session carefully. Now that you have accumulated a significant amount of information about the dynamics of distinctive operating styles, you will have the opportunity to be detective and counselor. Here are the facts.

Kent Stevens is a teenager whose operational style has always had him going down unique paths. He wore his hair long when everyone else wore theirs short. Then he had it all cut when it became fashionable to have long hair. The more formal his friends' attire, the more casual were Kent's clothes. And when his friends began to wear informal clothes, Kent developed a sudden affinity for neckties, visiting Salvation Army thrift stores to see what Ivy League cravat he could add to his collection.

Kent's stories for English class had incredible plot twists. He found novel ways to get his heroes in and out of scrapes. When he tired of that, he tried to write a five-page story where he could put the five pages in any order and still have the story make sense. Later he asked his teacher's permission to write a script for an assignment and produce a videotape production. Permission granted, he corralled a number of his friends to be actors and solicited others to help put it all together.

His mother describes how Kent, as a very young child, would be intrigued with a toy and spend a lot of time playing with it. Then one day he would suddenly put it aside and invest his attention in another. This new focus of attention would keep him occupied until he would exhaust its novelty and then move on to another one. Not every toy appealed to him—only those which could be reshaped into different forms or used for building a variety of structures.

Kent has a lot of friends of all ages. He gets along with adults by asking a seemingly unending series of questions about their work and hobbies. Everybody seems to like him. The only person who has doubts about Kent is his father. The two do not seem to get along too well.

Kent's father, Mr. Stevens, is an engineer known for his thoroughness. In his company, he is the last man to approve any design project before it is released. He is respected by the nine people who work directly under him. They appreciate the fact that each person knows exactly which part of the project he is responsible for. They know that by following directions to the letter, the specific components for which they are responsible will be ready at the time they are needed to fit into the total project.

Mr. Stevens is considered an excellent people person. The number of his employees who had to be transferred or fired was low compared to other departments within the company. He not only made a point of providing his engineers with clear goals, but he provided them with the directives which would enable them to achieve those goals. As a result productivity was high, and Mr. Stevens made a point of letting his people know how well they did and how he felt about their contribution.

Anyone who knew Kent and his father would give a good report on both of them. Both are quality people. Yet a poor relationship exists between them with neither side knowing what to do about it.

Now it's time for you to make your recommendations. Answer the following questions according to what you have learned from your reading so far. If you need help, go back to the appropriate section of the book and review.

(1) What would you say is the source of the clash in the relationship between Kent and Mr. Stevens?

(2) How would you summarize the operating style of each one?

(3) What critical information should the father and son know about each other?

(4) How would you advise Mr. Stevens to get along better with Kent?

(5) What advice would you give Kent about how to adjust to his father's operating style?

(6) How important do you think it is that they make any adjustments at all? (Doesn't the father have the authority to operate the way he feels is best? Doesn't the son have the right to expect to be accepted the way he is?)

(7) How optimistic are you that this relational problem will be resolved? Explain your answer.

THEOLOGY OF FUN

In this chapter we want to discuss the last of our four categories of activities: expressive behavior. This category contrasts with the other three in that it doesn't take place to accomplish any specific goals. Nothing practical takes place when your child plays soccer, draws a picture, or turns cartwheels. He may experience side benefits like getting exercise or developing his motor/visual coordination, but these are not the reasons why your child expresses himself.

If you ask a child why he is doing something in this expressive category, in most cases he will say it is fun. If you push him further, he won't understand what you are asking. To him, it makes perfect sense to have fun for fun's sake—not because fun functions as a means to a deeper philosophical motivation. And the child's instincts are correct.

The justification for expressive behavior is realized in the experience of the activity. People who participate in sports, games, art, dance, music, and poetry do so because they like these activities—not because of other goals.

The universe is God's multimedia, multidimensional work of art. Like all works of art, it has no practical use. This is not to say that it has no importance, just that it has no utility.

Play is important for adults as well as children. Expressive behavior should be a lifelong pursuit. It is not a temporary activity for children.

Creation itself was an expressive action of God. Creating the world was not a utilitarian act because God had nothing practical to accomplish. It was not the result of a relational need because God wouldn't be God if He were incomplete in Himself. Creation was not a product of God's developmental behavior because He cannot develop. He is energetically the same—yesterday, today, and forever.

If we want to explore the reasoning behind God's creation, we can best explain it as His expressive behavior. It is one way that He has chosen to express Himself, just as we might choose to paint a landscape, write a poem, or play football.

So how does all this information relate to your child? First, we should guard against developing a diminished opinion toward expressive behavior. When we do, we diminish ourselves. Expressive behavior has great value. Our children, made in God's image, must discover that value if they are to fulfill God's will in terms of how they are created. And God builds a number of capabilities into each child. Play, roleplay, fantasy, games, and athletics are all possible when the mind and the imagination work together. A balanced educational program supplies the mind with opportunities to switch from development and utilitarian concerns to more expressive abilities.

Art is a deeper form of expressive behavior. It not only involves expression of individual feelings, but shares them with the community in concrete forms (drawings, writings, paintings, sculptures, dance, theater, mime, music, etc.). All children use artistic expression to convey ideas which cannot be communicated any other way. Yet many adults are cut off from whole worlds of understanding because of their failure to cultivate this aspect of their education.

We can see an example of this in the Bible, where the poetry of the Psalms and the Song of Solomon convey feelings about God which could not be expressed in any other way. Remember that the Bible is not written as a technical manual. In addition to history and doctrine is a wealth of creative expressive writing.

TRAINING THE CHILD TO BE EXPRESSIVE

Children will be naturally drawn to expressive activities which fit their own interests and strengths. Some, because of venturesome elements in their design, will tend to seek out the right activities on their own. Others will have a greater dependency upon opportunities which happen to come their way. Parents and teachers should provide resources to help the child in either situation.

A child's design is easily confirmed in most expressive situations because there are no rigid standards. Expressive activities provide an opportunity for abundant response because the child's unique qualities can be pointed out. This is obviously true in free play and art. But it is also true in more formalized sports.

For example, some sports-minded children are best suited to team sports while others prefer solo performance. A solo performer on a team will still operate like a solo performer. A baseball or soccer team may not be right for such a child, though he could still maintain his solo style on a wrestling, ski, or swim team.

In learning sports skills, one child learns how to hit by watching a good hitter, another by experimenting, and still another by studying books on baseball. Some children prefer sports that use their own bodies (swimming, wrestling, etc.) and other children are inclined to use equipment (hockey, lacrosse, tennis, etc.).

Use the following sections to organize your thoughts about what best fits your child in the areas of play, sports, and art.

Sports

Is your child best suited to be a team person, a solo performer, or on a team comprised of soloists?

Should your child be involved in a sport that involves equipment? Does this issue make any difference? How well would he take care of his equipment? What is his interest in the technology involved with the equipment?

What is the best way for your child to learn the skills involved? Observation? Repetition? Demonstration? Reading? Diagrams? Experimenting?

What kind of coaching is needed? Directive? Suggestive? Motivational? Challenging? Technical? Collaborative? Structured?

What kind of role is natural for your child? Performer? Expert? Star? Team leader? Team member? Competitive? Technician?

What does your child want to get out of the sport? An opportunity to win? The possibility of overcoming size limitations, gender restrictions, or other handicaps? A good physical workout? The highest score? A reputation? An opportunity to strategize? To beat his own time? To have the best form? Recognition? A trophy? Competition? To please the crowd? To take risks?

> Your responses to these questions should build on what you already know about your child's design. Once you have a clearer picture, you can act accordingly.

Play

What is your child's attitude toward play? A social opportunity? A group activity? A team activity? An independent activity?

Do your child's play activities require structure? Organization? Leadership?

Does your child improvise, or is there a need for manufactured toys or equipment?

Does he request equipment and materials, or does he make his own?

What kind of play does your child like best? Can he repeat the activity or does he prefer variety?

How does this play activity need end for your child to be satisfied?

Art

In what artistic area is your child interested? Words? Movement? Materials? Line? Color? Gesture? Characters? Roles? Situations? Environments?

Does his artistic activity require others? If so, who?

Does he prefer for his art to be a spontaneous activity? Planned? Structured? Casual? Formal?

Do opportunities need to be provided? Are lessons required?

What does the child want to do with his finished product? A public viewing? Appearance on the bulletin board at home? Praise from parents? Praise from experts? Applause? Meeting prearranged standards? An opportunity to discuss the results? Peer recognition?

Or is the child more interested in the actual process rather than the end results?

The Role of Parents

After evaluating your previous answers, what do you think would be your best plan of action as a parent? Consider which of the following roles would be good for you to play, if any.

____ No involvement needed other than affirmation

____ Need to attend the child's events

____ Should help him practice and develop skills

____ Should actively coach or manage the team

____ Need to be careful not to impose my desires into the situation

____ Need to provide ample exposure to opportunities

____ Need to help my child become independent in this area

____ Need to provide lessons, expert coaching, or advice

____ Need to provide recognition at home (display trophies, newspaper articles, etc.)

WORSHIP

The capacity to worship is universal in humankind. In spite of the many substitutes that man uses, the natural object of worship is God.

While we're on the subject of expressive behavior, we need to consider the topic of worship. While it is assumed that children will be exposed to formal worship in church settings, this is another area where the design of your child is very important. The better you know him, the better you can anticipate how he will respond to the church experience. With a little foresight you can provide the right buffers for the aspects of adult worship which are tedious for the child.

But more importantly, you need to be aware of another level of worship which is informal and very personal. Because of our unique capacities, each of us has a very specific ability to appreciate a particular aspect of God. In addition, we each tend to relate to other personalities in our own distinctive style. These two factors provide a script for the kind of communication possible between yourself and God.

People first need to see how God reveals Himself in their lives. Then they need to find the most natural way of responding that holds their enthusiasm. This type of communication with God can begin early in life. Parents should use their spiritual intuition in figuring out how to encourage personal worship, given the unique nature of their own child.

The parent's goal should be for children to experience God in an intimate way, remembering that God has an even stronger interest in such relationships then we do. Parents need to expect that God will enter into such situations. Such faith is not only a benefit for the parents involved, but also a model for the children. This model of faith may be the base that the child builds on as he or she matures into a caring, worshipful individual.

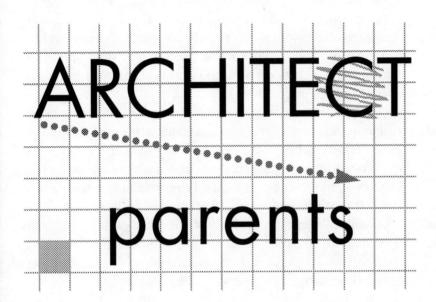

ARCHITECT parents

The role of parent is often difficult and overwhelming. But one of the places where it seems to be most appreciated is within Christian culture. The Bible holds the responsibility of parent in high regard. We are taught that the repercussions of parental influence not only affect all of one's life, but stretch into eternity itself. That is a sobering idea.

We have already considered the intense influence of the mother upon the child during the first year of life. This view is supported both by Scripture and extensive research. However, popular Christian culture may tend to place greater responsibilities upon parents than they are meant to bear. To illustrate this, we should consider the common view of *parents as architects.*

The parent as architect is not difficult to describe. Such parents believe that they will be totally responsible for what

Well-meaning parents, attempting to follow the commands of Scripture, sometimes become overly zealous architects of their child's design.

the child eventually becomes. The architect parent goes to a mental drawing board and designs the child from beginning to end. The design is usually so complete that it embraces all aspects of the child's life. Even physical appearance, over which the parent has no control, is addressed in terms of how the child's looks will be packaged and presented.

Regardless of whether the architect parents are blue-collar workers or university graduates, they will develop a clear image of the "package" that they expect their child to become. Architect parents are careful about the toys they buy—whether plastic guns and commando troops or the latest thing in developmental toys. They know that these toys will influence the minds of the child who plays with them. Some architect parents are deliberate in teaching their kids to be peacemakers and avoid fighting at all costs. Others encourage children to protect their rights.

Architect parents are also careful about what they allow their children to be exposed to. Some steer children toward books and ballet, others to guns and fishing rods. In either case, the parents are careful to indoctrinate their children into a particular value system. They make sure the children play with the right playmates and socialize with what the family thinks are their kind of people.

When a child of architect parents grows up, the parents still have clear expectations as to what that individual should do with his or her life. Depending on the family, the child might be expected to become whatever Dad is, enter some kind of ministry or service, get a good job, get married, raise a family, get all the education possible, or make a lot of money. Whatever the parent's intent might be, the child knows precisely what is expected and will experience extraordinary guilt if he pursues any other path. After all, it is the architect who really knows the total design. Whenever architect parents are also Christians, they often justify their intentions with spiritual or biblical principles.

> The intended shape of the child can be quite varied. The common characteristic of architect parents is that they have a clear mental model of what they want the child to become.

Some architect parents act the way they do because it fits the way they are designed. They simply do what comes naturally, and it is natural for them to want to control other people's lives. Other architect parents do what they do because they believe it's what good parents *ought* to do. They spend much energy in self-discipline, attempting to make sure the child turns out all right. They go to seminars and read books. They try to know exactly how their child is going to look, speak, act, and think.

Of course, this portrayal of architect parents is a stereotype. Yet sometimes it takes such an overstatement to help us to identify a well-disguised problem. The mind-set of architect parents is supported to a great degree by the training processes of the church. Christian culture is very partial to models that can be imitated. And while sometimes models are helpful, they tend to smother the creative power that drives healthy societies.

It is natural for parents to look for role models. They want to do the best possible job as a parent, and they also want their kids to turn out right. Using a model seems to be a simple way to accomplish these desires, but there can be problems with using models. When we imitate someone's excellent example, our lives can take on a splendor that was previously absent. But we must be careful in the attempt to follow a model that we don't lose our own identities. God never intended for parents or children to conform to expectations which have little to do with the way He designed them.

It sounds almost comical to describe some of the stereotypes that Christian culture sometimes uses as models. One classic image is that of the Christian mother: a highly organized individual who has everything at home under control, is always understanding, never speaks an angry word, loves to cook, and finds interesting recipes to try out for dinners (which are always economical, nutritiously balanced, and on time for her husband's arrival). For

Architect parents feel guilty if their child deviates in any way from the preconceived norm that has been established for him or her.

Nor do the majority of Christian fathers regularly manage their time so they can spend hours playing baseball with their sons, repairing things around the house, and handling the family finances with the greatest of ease.

a majority of Christian families, such a description is far from reality.

For some reason, these unrealistic stereotypes often become the models that many Christians strive to imitate. While we know that no one *really* lives according to the models, we believe that we *ought* to. We ought to be supermoms and superdads. We ought to love everything about being a parent: repairing, cooking, balancing checkbooks, organizing, running the family taxi service, and reading to the kids whenever they ask. And we feel there must be something wrong with us if we do not exert the effort to become such people. While there is nothing wrong with improving our efforts to be good parents, it *is* wrong to spend many years trying unsuccessfully to become somebody other than we really are.

It's bad enough when parents consider themselves inadequate and are thereby cut off from any realization of success. But the situation gets worse if they pass along the problem to their children. We must be very careful not to lay expectations on our children which have little to do with how they are designed. If this happens, we duplicate in their lives the same sense of not quite making the grade.

The stereotype of an ideal child is one who is quiet, responsible, loving to brothers and sisters, clean, neat, always on time, faithful in completing homework assignments, creative in play, fair in sports, interested in academic study and in sermons, a good eater, responsible, and so forth. These expectations are based on common sense and conformity. None are unreasonable for people who have to live together in the same house with some degree of tranquility. Yet it is unrealistic for parents to expect children to display all of these characteristics all the time.

It is dangerous to have our children conform to every whim imposed on them. It causes them to become indecisive and spiritually weak, substituting a legalistic awareness of God for an enthusiastic knowledge of their Creator. They

What may be true in our culture won't necessarily apply in other places. In countries where water is scarce, the American daily shower seems like a waste of a valuable resource. But children in those countries will have other expectations which English-speaking nations might not understand.

are therefore driven to become right rather than holy. Holiness is never achieved by adherence to models or rules. Rather, the Holy Spirit brings it about through an intimate relationship. In this way, holiness is a state of being in God and behaving accordingly. Biblically, it should be the norm for all Christians, not just a selected few superspiritual people.

Many Christians have a misconception of what holiness should be. Very few see it as a matter of beautiful actions and relationships emerging out of an enthusiasm for serving God, displayed in day-to-day living. The reason for the misperception is that holiness has traditionally been taught by presenting a perfect model and pointing out our own shortcomings. But teaching holiness *should* be a matter of nurturing a unique relationship with God. Holiness must be taught by teachers who themselves have a unique relationship with God and know how to initiate (not indoctrinate!) others into such a relationship. There's no reason this teaching couldn't begin early in a child's life.

It's amazing that some of the people who spend the most time with the Bible seem to be least affected by the splendid diversity of its characters. While they seek to define the perfect pastor, the perfect parent, the perfect disciple, the perfect child, and the perfect Christian (so they can make duplicates), they miss the point that God announces Himself as the God of Abraham, Isaac, and Jacob. Think for a moment about the diversity of that set of characters. Isaac and Jacob were by no means spiritual clones of Abraham. Abraham's life of faith and submission was far different than Jacob's life-style of self-effort and deception. Yet each one served God in his own way, and the Lord was God of all three of them.

Your child may be nothing like what you desire or expect. That's OK. God has a very good reason for creating him in such a way. And unlike an architect building a structure, you won't be able to stop the process and adjust the

> **The church does pretty well in teaching rules of behavior to its people, but it seems confused about how to teach holiness.**

shape or color anytime you want to. You need to take a different approach as a parent, one that allows God to bring about unique results beyond anything you might have envisioned as an architect. That alternative approach is the subject of the next chapter.

Looking Toward HARVEST

If we discard the metaphor of parent as architect, what can we use in its place? To be honest, the replacement we suggest is not as stylish as the architect. In fact, there is a degree of ordinariness to it that might be quite refreshing. Consider the image of *parents as farmers.*

The farmer does not treat peaches like apples, nor cauliflower like pole beans. True, they all need the same basics—sunlight, good soil, fertilizer, water, and weeding. But they need differing degrees of each ingredient and different proportions of minerals in the fertilizer.

Though there is a basic collection of tools and machines used for all these crops, there are particular tools used only on certain crops. Above all, the farmer remains aware that he only nurtures what God is creating each day as the crops germinate, grow, flower, and eventually bear fruit.

The farmer is very active, but at the same time he is also the observer of what God is doing. He is in partnership with God.

WHEN TO BE ACTIVE, WHEN TO BE PASSIVE

The idea of a partnership in farming is a strong one. We realize that not much will happens if the farmer doesn't throw himself wholeheartedly into bringing crops to fruition. That's his responsibility, and all his efforts lead to a productive harvest. But it is equally true that nothing happens at all if God doesn't do His part. The farmer works with an absolute dependence on God to provide sun and rain. Even the farmer who does not believe in God knows, too well, the limitation of his powers.

The active farmer wants pears to be pears, spinach to be spinach, avocados to be avocados, and peas to be peas. He rejoices in the identity of what is planted and does everything to nurture each crop according to its own nature. How silly it would be if a farmer with a magnificent apple orchard decided that he wanted pears instead. He could experiment with different fertilizers, prune differently, change the amount of water, or put different labels on the trees, but all he is going to get are apples. Taken to the extreme, this farmer's misguided efforts could even destroy the conditions in which apples flourish, and he could end up with trees that bear neither pears nor apples. All his hard work would be for nothing.

While farmers are highly active in the nurturing of their crops, they must also learn to yield to circumstances over which they have no control. In the full knowledge of God's splendid grace, they must sometimes face the inexplicable. They watch as seeds that were carefully planted with excitement and hope are washed away by floods. They see a promising, vigorous crop destroyed slowly and surely by drought. During many of these times, all they can do is passively observe.

When the romanticism of the farm disappears so that it is no longer a scene of fruitfulness, the farmer becomes vulnerable to bitterness and severe disappointment. Impotent to bring about what clearly would be best for all of us, he

> Where orchards are concerned, it is a shame that no fruit is produced where there could be an abundance that blesses the tree, the farmer, and all those who buy the apples. Where humans are involved, the situation is tragic.

faces the choice of fighting the unbeatable or embracing the tragic nature of it all. Siding with Job, he states, "Though He slay me, yet will I hope in Him" (Job 13:15). By these words the farmer confesses his hope in Jesus Christ who bore impossible burdens of futility and loss, saw beyond the spent tears and blood, and knew that ultimately in God there is no tragedy.

Similarly, we as parents survey our weaknesses. We repeat our parents' mistakes as we treat our children according to what was done to us. We recognize our ignorance and stupid actions. But we know that God can sweep it all up in the terrible wonder of redemption and give us power to be all He intends.

God invented parenthood. It was His idea that new personalities be brought into being through our participation as parents. We are engaged to a God who determined that children be conceived in the midst of passion. It should not surprise us to realize that, with more intensity than we can ever know, God's passion for us presses us from all sides. He is for us. He is for each of our children. He is champion of their lives, their years, their health, their calling, and their eternal destiny. Why not cooperate with what He intends?

Don't forget: Parenthood was God's idea.

It may be your purpose to help your child see the nature of God. But if you look closely enough, don't be surprised if you soon find that you are seeing God through the nature of your child. This wonderful experience is but one of the benefits you will receive if you dedicate yourself to the task of discovering your child's design.

APPENDIX

Whenever you examine human behavior, you will quickly realize that any action is driven by a complex combination of internal and external forces. Culture is an enormously powerful force, often restricting the scope of our ideas through the boundaries of the language we speak or the traditions we know.

Another powerful influence on an individual's actions is his opinion of his own worth. This factor can set one person free to take on goals others merely daydream about, while imprisoning another in a bleak, unfulfilling job.

Other major influences include education, religion, family life, history, and genetics. Sometimes these complexities resist successful analysis. They can cause significant changes in an individual's life. Yet these influences cannot prevent the discovery of certain long-term consistencies of behavior which can be applied to day-to-day living.

Every individual is influenced by an almost incomprehensible intertwining of forces.

MEANINGFUL THEMES

Most people recognize certain rhythms in the way they operate. Yet too often our observations are fragmented and are viewed through the window of emotional and psychological factors. We fear certain things, people, or situations. We may see ourselves as insecure. We have too much or too little pride. We don't trust other people. The list goes on and on. When internal and external forces continue to bombard each other in chaotic confusion, some people give up trying to make sense of it all.

The best way to bypass chaos is to concentrate on the moves an individual makes in life which are *not* unclear, and which can be judged as essentially likable. The stories people tell about the enjoyable things they have done are valuable because they reveal consistent themes which, in turn, yield knowledge to help the people make wise decisions in the future. These stories result in objective data. Psychoanalytical explanations for the same behavior, however, cannot be so easily validated.

Certain consistencies in operating style can be perceived when individuals tell stories about what they like and dislike, where they devote their time and energy, what things attract them, and for what they have an affinity. It's easy enough to tell if a person's stories have consistency. When someone tells stories from various phases of his or her life where every story contains an action initiated under the influence of a leader, you have a consistent fact that you can work with. An occasional mention of something should not be considered consistent.

The integrity of this approach is realized when consistencies from personal history allow the person to gracefully arrive at irrefutable conclusions. This process lets the person go beyond mere recognition of isolated skills to perceive a tapestry of personality in which each identified thread is related to the other threads comprising the total design.

Even though psychology can be used for understanding behavior, it doesn't help much in regard to practicalities of job fit, education, management, and child rearing.

To discover an individual's consistent style of operating, you don't compare his behavior to an objective standard, as would be characteristic of most methods of testing. When you truly believe each individual is unique, there will be no standard to which you can compare him. Rather, you should attempt to discover and piece together his consistent behavior and expect him to confirm your results. This needs to be done systematically so you can understand what has been previously perceived only in fragments. It's like giving someone a vocabulary to clearly express what he has only vaguely glimpsed from time to time.

LIKES AND DISLIKES

Everybody has stories to tell about their lives. Some are quite positive and others aren't. In the discovery process, not every story will be useful. A useful story will describe a particular move made by the storyteller. In addition, the action must be one they liked, at least for the most part. This exercise provides the history in which the evidence of the storyteller's interests and gifts are contained.

Why the emphasis on having the person tell stories of something he or she *liked* to do? Liking or disliking something is so natural to us that we do not see its significance, but a person's preferences reveal a lot. We chalk up our likes and dislikes as a matter of personal taste. Taste, in turn, is perceived to be merely a product of one's upbringing—how one is educated and how well-traveled he is. And many of these factors are determined by our culture. Therefore, the things we like may actually reveal much about the way we have been conditioned.

Let's use food as an example. If we have studied a wide variety of cultural customs from different geographic locations, our logic tells us that eating a fat grub in the Amazon is not much different than eating the muscles of a chicken in an expensive American restaurant. Yet if we were ever force-fed a three-inch grub, our logic might fly

First-person descriptions of specific, enjoyable experiences make the best stories when evaluating someone's distinctive operating style.

out the window as our cultural mores began to exercise a great deal more power over us. The episode would likely be concluded by involuntarily throwing up all that had been forced down. Such is the power of culture over logic.

Culture influences, and may even determine, many of our preferences. Yet a person's culture does not explain all of the moves he makes throughout his life. The unique personality of the individual is always expressed by many of his actions, the motivation behind them, and the style in which they are carried out. Such factors often override cultural influences, and are consistent.

Individuals reveal their consistencies in the stories they tell about things they have liked doing. The situations might have be difficult, stressful, or even unpleasant. But if the person liked the result of the experience, the story is an important one.

CATEGORIZING ENTHUSIASM

Behind the simple categories of *like* and *dislike* is an organized picture of an individual's enthusiasms. The word *enthusiasm* comes from the Greek *entheos,* meaning "that which is inspired by God." Another appropriate synonym for enthusiasm might be "arousal."

Man has been given the capacity to ardently attach himself to a cause, object, or pursuit. He does not carelessly choose to be involved, but something from within him inspires interest, zeal, fervor, or even passion. Therefore, it is characteristic of the human personality to have enthusiasm for only certain objects or pursuits.

The most mysterious capacity about a person's enthusiasm is that it allows him to make certain choices that influence the shape of his personality. This tendency develops in a consistent way and probably is as unique as any other portion of the human configuration.

Enthusiasm has an object in every case. The object may be abstract (such as an original idea) or concrete (a

Of two children in the same family, one might like to work with numbers and the other one won't. The fondness for numbers (or lack of it) goes beyond culture to reflect an inherent affinity—a personal preference.

Enthusiasm is the key word in understanding the strengths and gifts of individuals because it describes what fills or inspires them.

book, person, situation, or condition). In either case, enthusiasm is processed in the context of the influences of culture and experience. So we may say that enthusiasm is dependent on two sources of power: (1) the God-given precondition from within, and (2) the context—objects or situations toward which one is drawn from without.

Is there a connection between the two sources of our enthusiasm? In a sense, yes. It is as if God, who inspires from within, has shaped us with inner chambers which only certain external forms can occupy. The same God has shaped the outer forms, some of which will naturally fit into those chambers. And just as we know the reality of that which propels us from within, we also know the power inherently residing in those objects we consider meaningful to us.

In relationships a man can be described as "making a move" toward a woman to whom he is attracted. He does not move toward just any woman, only those who exhibit very specific qualities. He would agree if we described him as needing to relate to a particular kind of woman (internal forces). He would also concur that he is drawn only to particular woman (external influences). The way we move in social and vocational situations are not unlike the man's "moves" we have just described. The difference is that our culture has taught us to identify the dual source of influence in sexuality, but not in the other cases.

When we recognize the nature of these powers which influence our actions, our individual personalities become dynamic instead of static. And since the personality is continually developing, we can make certain assumptions about the enthusiasms of a fifteen year old and of that same person twenty years later. First, we will see consistency—enough so we can easily tell that this is the same person. Second, we will usually see evidence of vigorous development. The degree and the quality of development will depend on the two internal factors of predisposition and

Whether we are considering issues of personality, sex, esthetics, spiritual development, vocation, or whatever, each individual has the capacity to be enthused by particular situations or objects because of his unique design.

We are taught that we can't marry just any person without taking a serious gamble on the relationship. Yet we are told that it's OK to marry ourselves to any job that pays enough.

character plus the four external forces of opportunity, culture, education, and upbringing.

DECISION MAKING

Yet in spite of all the consistencies and developmental expectations of a person's life, these unchangeable forces do not drive the individual toward an inevitable end. A person has the capacity to bring about change and to enhance the quality of his life on all levels.

Though change and development take place, they are not predetermined by fixed causal forces (the concept behind the Greek Fates). Nor do they allow the individual to arrive at any given possibility. If this were the case, we would have to believe that decision making has no particular objective. The individual's power to decide works within the limitations of each situation and is affected as well by his internal and external influences.

When a person is given the power to make decisions, other influences are added to the ones previously mentioned. The person's enthusiasm is still the most dynamic source, but is strongly supported by logic and intuition. None of us are ever in a pure state of freedom to choose anything. We must always work with inherent limitations that come from our enthusiasms and the specific time and circumstances of each decision.

Most day-to-day decision making is driven by the power of logic. This quality is in no way diminished by the absence of enthusiasm.

CHARACTER

When we recognize the power of our internal and external influences, we realize that we don't decide to which things we will be attracted. But we do make decisions about how we respond to those attractions. We choose to make a move that can be either bad or good. We are not programmed to do one thing or the other. Such a condition would reveal a weak character and an absence of choice.

Rather, we can know what *ought* to happen and make appropriate choices to get to that point. The inability to make such choices can be corrected, if necessary, through the intervention of counselors, community, or God. The benefit of effective decision making is freedom. And the ultimate goal of freedom is to allow you to become the person God has designed you to be.